MASSACRE IN CUMBRIA

MASSACRE IN CUMBRIA

THE DAY GUNMAN DERRICK BIRD BROUGHT TERROR TO THE LAKE DISTRICT

CLARE LEIGH

JOHN BLAKE

Published by John Blake Publishing Ltd,
3 Bramber Court, 2 Bramber Road,
London W14 9PB, England

www.johnblakepublishing.co.uk

First published in paperback in 2010

ISBN: 978-1-84358-294-6

British Library Cataloguing-in-Publication Data:

A catalogue record for this book is available from the British Library.

Design by www.envydesign.co.uk

Printed in Great Britain by CPI Bookmarque, Croydon, CR0 4TD

1 3 5 7 9 10 8 6 4 2

Papers used by John Blake Publishing are natural, recyclable
products made from wood grown in sustainable forests.
The manufacturing processes conform to the environmental
regulations of the country of origin.

Every attempt has been made to contact the relevant
copyright-holders, but some were unobtainable. We would be grateful
if the appropriate people could contact us.

CONTENTS

PROLOGUE

West Cumbria, June 2010

On a beautiful, early summer morning there are few regions in the British Isles that can compare with West Cumbria. With its valleys and fells, views of the Irish Sea, picturesque hamlets and villages, the fading but still splendid grandeur of its Victorian seaside resorts – and of course the Lake District itself – it is little wonder that this region is one of the most popular tourist destinations in the United Kingdom.

As a county it has much to offer the visitor. For the rambler and the walker, there are its imposing and magnificent fells. The nature lover will adore its national parks, while the artist will be captivated by the landscape itself. Families come time and time again to enjoy a traditional English seaside holidays at one of its intriguing old resorts – Seascale, St Bees, Alloby and Silloth being favourites. Those with a love of history flock to Hadrian's Wall and to other Roman sites, such as the fort at Maryport or the fortlet at Crosscanonby. And those who simply want to enjoy a bit of peace and quiet come to the Lake District, one of the most tranquil and beautiful parts of the country, and take a room in one of its pubs and inns, or rent a cottage.

But there is another reason why visitors always return to Cumbria, and it has nothing to do with its landscape, heritage or the fact that it is a place of outstanding natural beauty; it is because of the people themselves. For Cumbrians are known for their warmth, kindness, and their strong sense of community... a trait, some might argue, that has all-too-sadly disappeared from other parts of England over the years.

So on a hot morning in the early summer of 2010, when the schools were off for a week and children were enjoying the half-term break, visitors from all around the country had flocked to Cumbria in droves. They went walking over the fells, took drives through the stone-walled lanes, and basked in the sunshine on the beaches.

And for the residents of this area too, 2 June, 2010 was set to be a good one. As they opened the curtains that morning and saw the haze rise up towards a brilliant blue sky it must have given them a sense of hope for finally, after months of one of the coldest and greyest winters in the history of the United Kingdom and the most unpromising of springs, summer seemed to have arrived at last. So as they set about their business, carried out their chores, and went about their daily routines there must have been smiles on many of their faces, and the faintest of springs in their steps.

The lawyer kissing his wife goodbye, before getting into his car and heading off for a day full of meetings; the cab driver, puffing on a cigarette in the sunshine in between fares, the mole catcher out with his dogs giving a helping hand to a farmer; the retired army man must have been enjoying his morning walk to the bookmakers; the parishioner out to meet her husband who was walking back from the newsagents; the former rugby player trimming the hedges on his family's farmland; the cyclist taking his daily bike ride along the coastline. All of these people must have felt cheered by the sun on their faces as they went about their routines. There were others who were enjoying the morning sunshine: the woman out delivering catalogues; the mother-of-two carrying her shopping home; the estate agent driving back to his office from a viewing. As these good people looked at the sky that morning, they all must have thought what a beautiful day it was.

But for all its natural beauty and its warmth of spirit, West Cumbria has had its fair share of tragedy in recent times. In 2009 the county had fallen victim to some of the worst floods in history. Heavy rainfall destroyed many people's homes, roads became rivers, and a bridge collapsed and in the process claimed the life of a respected police officer, PC Bill Barker. He had not only been a highly valued member of the local police force, as such both well known and liked within the community, but had been a dedicated family man too. 'A wonderful husband and devoted father' was how his wife chose to remember him at his funeral at their church in Egremont, which was attended by hundreds of mourners.

Then in May 2010 tragedy struck again when a coach carrying teenagers from Keswick School crashed on the A66 and tipped onto its side, after it collided with another vehicle. The 49-seater coach was transporting children from school back to their homes in Cockermouth, 13 miles away. Two children died in the crash: Kieron Goulding, just 15 years old, and Chloe Walker, who had been celebrating her 16th birthday that day.

Many of the surviving children were badly injured and most, it would be accurate to say, were left extremely traumatised. With two young lives cut short and so many injured, even the emergency services said they found it a difficult situation to deal with, as did the rest of community, who were shocked and saddened by the tragedy. But as Chief Inspector Kevin Greenhow from the Cumbrian Police said, 'The people of West Cumbria are resilient people and they will gather round and support each other.'

And that they did. For whilst the sun may have shone brightly on the morning of 2 June, some members of the community would have other things on their minds than merely the weather: this was the day that Chloe's family, who had already lost their son Jordan in 2007, were due to lay their daughter to rest. Family, friends and classmates were to attend her funeral and local people came out of their houses and lined the streets in a mark of respect and as a sign of solidarity towards these people. This is what West Cumbrian folk are like: strong, supportive, resilient, mindful and caring of others.

And so even as they went about their daily business on that morning, whether it was heading off to a meeting, driving a passenger across town, collecting the shopping or walking across the farmland, Chloe Walker and her family would not have been far from their thoughts. Especially sympathetic would have been those who had children of their own.

But whilst Chloe Walker may have been uppermost in the thoughts of the people of West Cumbria that morning, by the early hours of the afternoon there would be another name that would be etched into their minds, like an indelible stain: Derrick Bird.

For on the morning of 2 June, Derrick Bird, a self-employed taxi driver from the village of Rowrah, would single-handedly stage one of the most deadly massacres this country has seen for 14 years, taking the lives of twelve much-loved, respected and innocent people as he rampaged around the county, shooting his victims in cold blood.

Not since Michael Ryan shot dead 16 people on the streets of Hungerford, Berkshire, in the summer of 1987, or Thomas Hamilton walked into a primary school in his home town of Dunblane in Scotland, killing 16 children and their teacher, has there been such a brutal mass shooting in the United Kingdom. As in the killings of Ryan and Hamilton, Derrick Bird had taken the lives of the innocent. And, just like the Hungerford and Dunblane mass murderers, he had done so within a community that was said to be tight, close-knit and caring.

He would begin his spree at around 5:30am with the murder of his twin brother and he would end it, having taken the lives of eleven others and injuring twenty-five more, by finally turning his gun on himself eight hours later.

CHAPTER ONE

Ask any of Derrick Bird's neighbours who lived alongside him in the tiny hamlet of Rowrah what kind of person he was and invariably they will paint a portrait of a kind, decent, quiet, if slightly unassuming, man. 'Affable', 'neighbourly', 'friendly' and 'good natured' are the adjectives you will hear time and time again. His colleagues from the taxi rank in Duke Street, Whitehaven, where the cab driver plied his trade, and his drinking pals from the local pubs he frequented, would say the same thing.

He was a 'typical Cumbrian,' a 'good neighbour', a 'placid man' who 'kept himself to himself,' and yet also, conversely, one who could be a 'bit of a laugh' and 'good company'. Hardly epithets one would normally associate with the stereotypical profile of a mass murderer. For

1

Derrick Bird was apparently not a 'loner', an 'oddball', or a man with a violent temper. Instead, according to those that knew him, he was a sociable, mild-mannered and genial fellow.

He was also a family man – a father with two sons, who had, only recently, become grandfather for the first time – who cared for his elderly mother. He had a network of friends around the county as well as colleagues and neighbours with whom he was largely on good terms. He had hobbies and interests and he enjoyed going on holiday. On the face of it there was nothing particularly untoward about Derrick Bird. Little wonder then that in the days that followed the dreadful events of 2 June 2010 there was such a universal sense of disbelief around the West Cumbrian community that Derrick Bird could be capable of committing such atrocious crimes.

In the days following the shootings people who knew Bird simply weren't able to reconcile the memory of the man they knew and liked with the portrait of a cold-blooded killer that was now being presented to them by the media. According to them he was just an ordinary man. It was a 'different Derrick Bird', a 'stranger', who had stepped out of his house that morning on his murderous mission, killing twelve respected members of their community and seriously injuring eleven others. It was so 'out of character', as would be shown in the testimonials people would give in the following days.

'I can't believe he would do that – he was a quiet little fellow,' Sue Matthews, a telephonist at A2B Taxis in Whitehaven, would say. She had known Bird through work for many years and was stunned by the news. 'He was self-employed but A2B Taxis is a small place,' she explained. Peter Leder, a fellow cab driver and long-term friend would agree. In his eyes Bird was 'an outgoing, well-known guy who everyone liked.'

Ryan Dempsey, 26, a neighbour from Rowrah, who lived just two doors away from Bird and had known him since he was a child, described him as being warm and friendly, an 'easy-going sort of fellow'. 'He never walked past without saying hello,' he said. Dempsey had seen Bird just a couple of days before the shootings and he had seemed in a 'happy' mood, waving at him through the window and smiling.

Michelle Haigh, the landlady at the Hound Inn in Frizington, where Bird liked to drink, remembered him as a 'nice' and 'normal bloke'. 'He would come to the pub, have a couple of pints of lager, have a chat with his friend and go home,' she remembered. 'This is not in character with the Derrick Bird we know. Everybody is shocked.'

In the interviews given by friends and family immediately after the events of the second of June a picture would emerge of an 'ordinary man, living an ordinary life'. There seemed nothing exceptional about Derrick Bird. He was 52 years old, slightly short and tubby in stature, with thinning hair. He had lived his entire life in West Cumbria and for the past 16 years had resided in the hamlet of Rowrah in a small, modest and unassuming house. He had worked for more than 20 years as a self-employed cab driver, stationed at the rank in the main road of the former industrial town of Whitehaven.

These people, rightly or wrongly, believed they knew Derrick Bird, that they had the measure of him. They may have had their moments with him, for no one is without fault after all, but no one, for one second, could ever have imagined that Derrick Bird – their friend, their neighbour, their colleague, their drinking companion, their family member – was a potential killer, let alone a multiple murderer.

So who was Derrick Bird, the man who was affectionately known to many that knew him as 'Birdy'?

Derrick and his twin brother David were born in 1957 to Mary and Joseph Bird, a couple who were held in high regard within their local community. The boys and their older brother Brian, now 58, were raised in Ennerdale Bridge, a small and friendly village, which spans the River Ehen. It was the kind of place where everyone knew everyone and the Birds lived in a house, situated next to the local pub, that had been in the family for two generations.

Joseph, or Joe as he was known to family and friends, was popular and convivial, a stalwart of Ennerdale, who liked village life, often stopping off to chat to neighbours as he walked through the streets. Joe was proud of his Cumbrian roots, so much so that he spoke the dialect and often appeared on radio shows in the area, discussing local issues. He had met his wife Mary during the Second World War when she was working as a land girl and the couple had married soon afterwards. According to a former teacher who taught the twins, the Birds were a 'good family'.

Joe was employed by the council as a road worker. Typical of the time, Mary had stayed at home in order to raise her three sons and by all accounts they had a comfortable and happy childhood. Neighbours said that kind and upstanding Mary was much admired within the community and was an exemplary mother, one who was always there for her boys.

The boys attended the Ennerdale and Kinniside Church of England School at primary level and were later sent to Ehenside School, in Cleator Moor. Neither of the twins was especially academic but nevertheless they got on well at school. Their former teachers remember both David and Derrick as 'lively' and 'spirited' lads. Although they might have got up to mischief from time to time, neither boy was considered troublesome. Their interests lay outside the classroom – they were both fascinated by cars, an obsession they would carry into adulthood. For David this meant pursuing a career as a mechanic and garage owner. For Derrick it was manifested in a love of Motocross, a passion he would later pass on to his own son, Graeme.

But it was in the great outdoors, the astoundingly beautiful surroundings of the Cumbrian countryside, that the twins and their elder brother, Brian, seemed happiest. Joe, a countryman through and through, was a wildlife expert with an extensive knowledge of animals and birds, and he would regularly take the boys on hikes across the Ennerdale Valley at weekends, visiting the local lakes, exploring the forests or lamping for rabbits. Joe was a keen shot and, like many men in the area, kept licensed guns which, on his death in 1998, he would bequeath to Derrick.

At the age of 16 both twins left school, David taking on a mechanic's apprenticeship and Derrick finding work as a joiner. Both men went on to fall in love and forge relationships early on in life. David married Susan in 1980, the mother of his three daughters, whilst Derrick set up home with his childhood sweetheart, Linda Mills, whom he had met at secondary school. They went on to have two sons: Graeme, in 1985, and Jamie, in 1994. Derrick and Linda separated shortly after the birth of their second child.

It is common knowledge that the couple hadn't parted on the best of terms, but that didn't stop Derrick from maintaining contact – and a good relationship – with both of his sons. He made regular trips to the village that Linda Mills had moved to, Lamplugh, to visit his younger son, and he enjoyed watching Graeme compete in Motocross trials around the county. Indeed, just days before the shootings Derrick had spent at enjoyable afternoon watching his elder son take part in an event at Bassenthwaite Lake.

So, despite the fact that Derrick didn't live with his sons following his separation, he was close to both boys. He was said to have been pleased and reassured that his younger son Jamie was studying hard for his GCSEs and at Graeme's wedding to his wife Victoria, less than two years before the killing spree, Derrick was photographed posing in his morning coat and buttonhole, beaming with pride. In another picture, standing next to his brother Brian with a pint of beer in hand, he appears to be in a jovial mood.

On May 22 his daughter-in-law gave birth to a son, Leighton, and Derrick was immensely proud that he had just become a grandfather. According to his cousin, Joy Ryan, he was 'chuffed to bits' about the new arrival, so much so that on 1 June, the day before his rampage, he visited their house in a quiet cul-de-sac in Cleator Moor, just four miles from Rowrah, and presented the couple with a 'financial gift' for Leighton. During that meeting he proudly cradled the baby in his arms.

This unlikely killer was also said to have a good relationship with his mother Mary, and would regularly stop by for tea with the 87-year-old widow. When she was hospitalised with a serious illness, Derrick and his brothers spent an afternoon at her house sprucing it up in anticipation of her homecoming. The three men did such a thorough job that Mary later joked with her local vicar that she could no longer find anything in her kitchen. On her release from hospital Mary's three sons visited her at home, and they would all sit down to a meal together.

It would be fair to say that Derrick Bird was not the most ambitious of people, but he was a man who had learnt a trade and, as such, could and should have done all right for himself. Having worked first worked as a joiner at an undertaker's business in Whitehaven he would go on to take a position, not far away, at the famous nuclear plant in Sellafield, which still is the single largest employer in the area. It was a career with prospects and he had liked it there. But it did not last: in 1990 he was abruptly dismissed from the plant having been convicted of stealing materials from his employer, receiving a 12-month suspended sentence in the process.

Whether it was a simple act of folly that drove him to steal from his employers, thus jeopardising his career, or a crime that was committed out of financial necessity, is uncertain; but what is clear is that Bird soon realised how hard it would be for him to find full-time employment again. It was then that he decided to become a cab driver, and joined the rank in Whitehaven.

As well as being passionate about cars, Bird was an excellent driver and, having lived in the area all his life, he had an intricate knowledge of the winding lanes that weave and zigzag around the villages, towns and fells of West Cumbria. He was able to point out the landmarks and beauty spots to tourists holidaying in the area and he was on first-name terms with most of his regular customers. As a result he rarely needed to ask for addresses when someone climbed into his cab after a night out in Whitehaven.

Although he worked hard and made money, the job was unlikely to ever make him rich. In recent years the recession had taken its toll within that industry and work was thin on the ground. Whilst Derrick was not on the breadline, like many of his colleagues he would complain about finding it hard to make ends meet. Certainly, there is no question that his circumstances were in striking contrast to those of his twin brother. Unlike Derrick, David had prospered over the years by way of a succession of business and property ventures. He was self-made and lived in a certain degree of style, owning an attractive and substantial farmhouse set in four acres of land on the outskirts of Lamplugh, the village where Linda Mills had settled following her separation from Bird.

Derrick's own home in Rowrah was a far more modest affair. A mid-terraced, pebble-dashed two-up, two-down property, it could hardly be described as 'desirable' and it was in desperate need of modernisation. But still, Derrick seemed to enjoyed life in Rowrah, and having been in residency there for some time, he was both a well-known and liked member of that small hamlet. He got on well with his neighbours, many of whom he had known since he first moved there, and there were never any complaints about him.

He would always raise a smile or a wave at his fellow residents when he passed them, often stopping off to engage in conversation. On sunny days they would see him sitting out in his doorstep, cup of tea in hand, and at weekends, even when it was raining, he would be found tinkering under the bonnet of his cab – a silver Citroen Picasso – or giving the car a thorough clean. According to Ryan Dempsey no one on the street had 'a bad word to say about him'. He was friendly, pleasant and would always dip into his pocket whenever there was a collection for charity. Another neighbour James Campbell, 68, said he never found 'fault with him', adding, 'He has always been all right as long as I have known him. I used to speak to him as he was coming and going. We would say hello and pass the time of day. He's always been a good neighbour and a nice man as long as I have known him.' Sarah Jackson, another Rowrah resident, would back this up, describing Bird as a 'quiet guy, from a good family'.

At the cab rank in Duke Street, Whitehaven, the sentiment was the same. 'Birdy', as he was known there, was a well liked and an appreciated member of the crew. And even in times when work was thin on the ground he would be found alongside the other drivers drinking coffee and 'simply having a laugh' when waiting for fares, 'joshing' with his fellow cabbies.

Derrick Bird was also a man who had interests and hobbies outside work. As well as his love for Motocross – he was often seen out-and-about sporting a speedway jacket – he was an avid diver and belonged to the Solway Sub-Aqua Club in the area. He is said to have excelled at diving and, as well as attending the club on a regular basis, he would frequently go diving with friends in the Wasdale Valley, part of the Lake District National Park. His passion for the sport would take him all over the world.

As a result of his interests he had a good social life and

he would go out drinking a couple of nights a week. As well visiting the Hound in Frizington, he patronised the Stork Hotel in Rowrah, and the John Paul Jones pub in Whitehaven. There he would meet up with friends and enjoy a 'pint or two' before heading home.

At least once a year, finances permitting, he would holiday with friends, either from work or from the scuba club. The destinations he favoured were warm and sometimes exotic. Thailand was a favourite destination of his, one that he had visited on numerous occasions with both friends from the diving club and his fellow cabbies. And there would be other trips too, to Lanzarote, Tenerife, Croatia and Egypt, where he would be photographed by his travelling companions basking in the sun upon the deck of a motorboat.

Derrick Bird was nice, friendly, charitable and sociable to those that knew him. On paper, there were few bad words that could be attributed to the 52-year-old. By some people's standards Bird, as a character, may have seemed a little unassuming, his life, though content, a little unremarkable. But did that really matter? He seemed to enjoy what he took from his work and social interactions and had much to live for by all accounts and seemingly went about his business without complaint.

In the days after the massacre the portrait that friends and family would present of Derrick Bird was of a nice, kind and quiet fellow. 'He was just ordinary,' a local would say. 'Not that there's anything wrong with that. I liked him for it.'

Derrick Bird may have gone to bed as an 'ordinary' man on the eve of that fateful morning, but by the end of the following day he would go down in history as one of this country's most notorious mass murderers.

CHAPTER TWO

In the early hours of Wednesday, 2 June 2010, Derrick Bird closed the door on his pebble-dashed house in Rowrah and drove three miles east to his brother David's farmhouse, High Trees, in the village of Lamplugh. He was armed with two weapons: a shotgun and a .22 rifle fitted with a telescopic viewer and a silencer.

It was still dark when he arrived at his brother's property but Bird knew his way around the place and, after parking his car, let himself into the house, knowing full well that the door would be unlocked. According to family and friends this was not unusual. With such a low crime rate in West Cumbria, few people ever bothered about such things. Bird gained access to the house via the back door and then climbed the staircase to the first floor, entered the bedroom where his brother lay sleeping, and shot him dead at point-blank range, using his .22 rifle and silencer. It was 5.30 in the morning.

The body of the 52-year-old father-of-three would be found hours later slumped next to his bedroom door, with his beloved Labrador dog, Jed, clearly distressed by his side. This tragic scene was described by John Hinde, a local farmer and close friend of David's, who discovered the body later that morning.

Having cold-bloodedly killed the brother with whom he had shared a womb, Derrick Bird left the farmhouse and got back in his silver Citroen Picasso and drove home to Rowrah, where he coolly went about his business that morning as if 'nothing had happened at all'. According to one neighbour who had seen him on the street that morning he was spotted cleaning his car at around 9.30am. They had assumed that he was getting ready for his shift at the cab rank in Duke Street, Whitehaven, and said good morning to him. Derrick Bird nodded back.

At 10am Bird was back on the road again but he wasn't heading to work; he was driving in the direction of the village of Frizington, to Mowbray Farm, where family lawyer Kevin Commons lived with his wife. Earlier that morning, possibly on his return from Lamplugh, Derrick Bird had been up to Commons's farmhouse to check it out. On the way back from the farm he encountered Iris Carruthers on the lane, who was taking a morning walk with her dogs. Carruthers, 49, knew Derrick Bird – not only had they been to school together but only the day before Bird had visited her shop for groceries.

Carruthers assumed that Bird must have been up to the farm to drop a fare off. She was near enough to the car to bid him good morning. 'He had his window rolled down and so I said "Hiya lad, you all right?"' she recalled. 'But he didn't speak. He seemed dazed, as if he was in another world. He kept looking straight ahead.' Unable to get a response, she walked on. It wouldn't be until later in the morning, when news of the shootings started to emerge, that she realised the significance of what she had witnessed.

When he reached Commons's house for the second time that morning Bird stationed his car in front of the home of a man he was hunting. He waited for Mr Commons to come out of the house. At 10.20am, when the 60-year-old finally did emerge from his front door, Bird shot him dead on his driveway. It is not known whether the two men exchanged words and, due to the fact that his house stood on a remote spot, at the end of a steep private lane, his body would not be found for several hours. Bird had not fitted the silencer to his gun and neighbours called the police when they heard the shots. A patrol car was dispatched in the direction of Frizington to investigate. Bird, who was on the move again, passed the officers as he took the road out of the village.

With David Bird and Kevin Commons now dead, Bird headed to Whitehaven town centre to seek out his next victim: fellow cab driver Darren Rewcastle. Darren was at one time a friend, whom Derrick wrongly suspected of having an affair with his ex-partner, Linda Mills. The two men had also recently argued over the issue of queue-jumping at the taxi rank in Whitehaven. The events that followed, encompassing the murders which took place between 10.33 and 11.35am during Bird's 45-mile rampage through the area, were to become known as the 'second phase of killings'.

Arriving at the taxi rank in Duke Street at 10.30am, Bird sought out Rewcastle, who was working the morning shift. His quarry was standing in a doorway, smoking a cigarette and drinking a cup of coffee. According to another driver, Bird called over to Rewcastle: 'Darren, here, I want you.' Hearing his name, Rewcastle turned towards Bird, and, as he did so, his friend shot him in the face. Darren died instantly.

Bird was out of his car and was walking round the town with his shotgun in hand. Former Royal Marine Dan Williamson, who has served in both Iraq and in Afghanistan, heard the shots and ventured out of the shop he had been visiting. He saw Bird on foot and says that the killer didn't seem to be in a particular hurry but that he did appear to be looking for someone. Williamson was confused as to what was going on, as he would tell Channel 4 later: 'If you see someone with a gun running around in [Afghanistan or Iraq] you know there's a problem. If you see someone with a gun in Whitehaven you don't know what's going on.'

Back in his car Derrick Bird slowly circled the town and it appears that he was targeting other drivers from the rank. He drove up beside Don Reed, another Whitehaven cabbie who was standing on the street, and aimed his gun in Reed's direction. Fortunately the cab driver, who believes he was simply 'in the wrong place at the wrong time', was able to dive out the way as the gun erupted, merely receiving shrapnel wounds. 'He caught me in the back, I went on the floor, then crawled along the taxi rank,' he says. Not realising that Rewcastle was already dead, the latest casualty managed to get to Rewcastle's side, aiming to help him. He says: 'I was going to apply first aid to Darren but when I saw Darren, Darren didn't have a face. He wasn't there. He was gone.'

While this was happening, Bird took aim at another cab driver, Paul Wilson, a man who had considered Bird a close friend. Wilson was walking down Scotch Street, past the Whitehaven police station. Bird drew up alongside his next potential victim and called out to him so that Wilson dropped down to talk to him through the open window – only to be confronted with the barrel of a gun. At first the startled cabbie thought that his mate and drinking partner was playing a joke on him. He was, it emerged, very wrong. Bird pulled the trigger – he was trying to kill him. Wilson recoiled, stunned, initially thinking that Bird had fired a blank. But the cartridge was live and the shot Bird had fired had skimmed his cheek.

'He called my name and I said hello,' Wilson explained afterwards. 'And then I heard a pop. It was only when someone said to me, "You've been shot", that I realised.' Wilson then put his hand to his face and, when he looked at it, saw that it was wet with his own blood.

Paul Wilson rushed to the police station, where he not only identified the shooter, but was able to give the officers Bird's mobile number. 'I told them he was a friend of mine,' he said. The police in the control room at the station were then able to relay the information to patrol cars around the county, as well as to give them a description and the registration number of the car.

It was at this point that someone tried to intervene, and another cabbie shouted at the gunman: 'What the [fuck] are you doing?' prompting Bird to speed on.

Having murdered the three men whom he felt had wronged him, and taken aim at two of his colleagues, the spree began in earnest. Derrick Bird was no longer sticking to his mental 'hit list' of those against whom he held a grudge. Now anyone who crossed his path was a potential victim.

Up the road from Scotch Street he called out to 15-year-old Ashley Gastor, trying to lure her to his car. He asked the schoolgirl, who at the time was simply going to the local shop to run an errand: 'Do you want something?' As she leaned towards the vehicle to ask what he meant she saw the shotgun aimed at her and dropped to the ground, narrowly avoiding the blast – it came so close that she felt the shot whistle past her ponytail.

While she was getting to her feet in an attempt to flee, Bird aimed at her again but fortunately she was able to dodge his fire as she ran towards her sister and to safety. But as she escaped, all the teenager could think was: *What was the reason for this stranger to be shooting at me?* 'I kept thinking "why's he going to kill me?"' she said later. 'I've not done anything wrong.'

Like his other targets, the schoolgirl had assumed that the driver of the Citroen had simply stopped her to ask for directions; it never occurred to her that by offering to help she would come face-to-face with an assassin. 'He was pointing a gun at me through the window,' she described the scene. 'I put my hands over my head and ducked down to protect myself and the gun was fired.'

The police were now on Bird's case but with most of their officers four miles away in Frizington at the first reported murder scene there were few patrol cars in the Whitehaven area. Instead, an unarmed officer managed to commandeer a local cab, and the policeman and the driver went in pursuit of Bird. They were to be joined by another two policemen, again unarmed, in a police transit. Both vehicles chased Bird for a quarter of a mile around the one-way system, until they witnessed another shooting.

At Coach Street, Bird pointed his gun at Terry Kennedy, another taxi driver, who had passenger Emma Percival in the front of the car with him. Bird drew up to their car, pointed the barrel of the gun at them and fired. Kennedy didn't realise he had been shot until he turned to Percival and saw she was covered in 'flesh and blood'. Kennedy's right hand was so badly wounded that doctors were later forced to amputate.

Witnessing what had happened, the police rushed to their aid. Percival – who was also injured in her neck, arm and side – instinctively leapt from the car and, she later told the *Telegraph*, as she did so PC Mick Taylor shouted, 'Just run to me, lass!' Realising that Kennedy and Percival had survived, Bird attempted to come at them again, but as the police van had blocked his path, he sped off.

The police resumed their pursuit of the gunman but having tended to Percival and Kennedy they were now several minutes behind Bird and this delay caused them to lose him at a junction. At the control room in Whitehaven the police tried to contact Bird on his mobile phone but he wasn't picking up.

Having wreaked chaos in Whitehaven, Bird drove south along the coast. He was on the road to St Bee's but, aware of the fact that the police were chasing him, he changed his route, going cross-country through the market town of Egremont. It was here that he passed Susan Hughes at Haggett End. The 57-year-old mother of two, who had devoted her life to caring for her disabled daughter, had been shopping at her local Co-Op and was making her way up the steep hill towards her house, struggling with the weight of her grocery bags. According to a witness, when Bird spotted her he stopped the car, got out of it, and shot her twice in the stomach.

Barrie Moss, a local resident who was cycling past, saw Bird coolly walking back to the car holding what appeared to be a shotgun. 'It was like something out of a James Bond movie,' he reported. Moss looked back up the street and saw a body lying there with 'two shopping bags dropped to the ground'. He got off his bike and ran to Hughes's aid. She was still breathing but unconscious. 'Five minutes later she just stopped breathing and that was it,' he said. Stunned by what he had witnessed, it was only when a neighbour shouted out to him that there was 'a man on the loose' that he realised he had actually seen the killer.

By now it was 10.55am. Within just five minutes, at nearby Bridge End, Bird would come into contact with his next victim: 71-year-old Kenneth Fishburn, a retired soldier and former security guard at Sellafield. Fishburn was crossing the bridge over the River Ehen, on his way to the local betting shop. Bird shot him in the back and then drove off through the village firing his gun in the air.

In Egremont he was also to take aim at Les Hunter, who was visiting a friend in the village. The killer had called over to the handyman, saying, 'Have you got a minute mate?' As Hunter had leaned over into the car window to see what Bird wanted, the killer aimed the double barrel shotgun at his face. Luckily Hunter managed to turn his head away just in time – the pellets from the shotgun hit his cheek and ear, but he survived.

'I saw the shotgun and turned my head, meaning most of the pellets whizzed past my face. I have 39 pellets in my back,' he later explained to the *Sun* newspaper in an interview. 'If he had shot me the second time with his rifle and not the shotgun, I wouldn't be here.' Hunter would later attest that Bird seemed calm, he 'wasn't sweating' and 'didn't look like he was in a rush.'

Derrick Bird's most recent victims had been selected as

random killings but his next target wasn't. Jason Carey is an instructor at Bird's diving club, and a man against whom Bird bore a serious grudge. According to members of the Solway Sub-Aqua Club, Bird felt humiliated after Carey, quite rightly, had reprimanded him for irresponsibly taking a novice diver into deep water. The incident had seemingly scarred Bird and as a result he hated Carey 'intensely'. 'He would have got him if he could,' members of the club said. But fortunately for Carey, he was destined to escape death.

Arriving at Carey's front door at his home in Wilton, the would-be assassin banged on the door but Carey was still in bed, having worked a night shift. By the time his wife Deborah, who was struggling to restrain her barking dog, made it to the front entrance and opened it, Bird was already walking away. It had been a close call for Deborah; had she got to the door sooner both she and her husband would be dead.

Driving away from the Careys' house Bird passed farmer Norman Sherwen who was driving his tractor along the lane. He had expected Bird to slow down and greet him as he passed by – as was the country way – but Bird sped past him. Sherwen imagined that something must have upset Bird, that maybe he had been 'run off the road' and was in a 'foul mood', but said that he would 'never forget his face'.

Minutes later Sherwen heard a shot coming from the brow of the hill. Bird had claimed his next victim, taking the life of Isaac 'Spike' Dixon, a 65-year-old mole catcher, who, like the killer, had also worked at Sellafield, though it is not known whether the two men were known to each other.

Either way this appears to have been another random killing. Moments before, Dixon had been out walking his dogs and setting traps and was in conversation with a farmer. He simply had suffered the misfortune of being in the killer's path. Sherwen had known Dixon for most of his life. The pair had met as children, formed a lasting friendship, and attended each other's weddings, but now the man Sherwen later described as a 'good guy' and a 'friend' lay dead just 200 yards from his tractor.

By now all available police in the area, including 42 armed officers, had quite rightly been deployed to hunt for Bird. But perhaps due to the cab driver's extensive knowledge of the country lanes, he was always one step ahead of them. He would continue to elude his pursuers.

At 11.05am Bird was in the picturesque hamlet of Wilton, and came across Jennifer Jackson. The 66-year-old retired tax worker was a regular churchgoer and worked as the parish secretary and only that morning had been in conversation with the local rector about the recent coach crash, in which the two teenagers had died. Having gone to buy a newspaper she was walking along the lane to meet her husband James, or Jimmy, as he was known to his friends. When Bird's car pulled up James had been out getting some gentle exercise, having just recovered from a gallbladder operation. Once again the cab driver summoned a victim to his car, this time by sounding the horn. As Jennifer Jackson turned towards him he shot her dead.

At the time of the shooting, Jimmy, who was just

minutes up the road, was in conversation with neighbours Steve and Christine Hunter – a couple in their fifties, who had only recently moved to the area – on their doorstep at Town End Farm. Bird is said to have driven past the farmhouse, but after about 15 yards he reversed his car. The group assumed he was coming back to ask for directions but he shot at them through his open window. Steve Hunter managed to grab his wife and tried to swing her out of the line of fire, but she was shot in the back and would later suffer from a collapsed lung. Jimmy Jackson, hit in the head, fell to the ground and would later die from the gunshot wound.

'Bird never said a word throughout it all,' John Reed, a friend of the Hunters, said. 'Steve probably saved Christine's life by managing to move her out the way.'

It was now 11.10am and Derrick Bird had killed seven people. He had known three of them but the other four were strangers, who had simply been going about their daily business. It was nearly an hour since police had first got word of the fact that there was a gunman in the area, but they still couldn't seem to catch him. Without a helicopter unit of their own the Cumbrian police force would have to call in both the RAF and the Lancashire force to come to their aid. In the meantime the nuclear plant at Sellafield would be locked down – just as Bird passed it on the road.

Driving south towards the seaside town of Seascale, Bird was shooting now at anyone he came into contact with. Five minutes later in Gosforth, Bird gunned down Garry

Purdham. The 31-year-old was immensely popular and well known in the area, since he was a semi-professional rugby player. He was out trimming hedges on his father's farmland when he encountered Bird. The killer got out of the car, walked up to Purdham and shot the father-of-two in the head.

Word was spreading fast of a killer loose on the rampage. Television and radio stations gave rolling news reports on the shootings, urging the people of West Cumbria to stay indoors on the advice of the police. They named the killer as Derrick Bird; a 'local man' who was both 'armed' and 'extremely dangerous'. In the meantime the Cumbrian Police sent out urgent public messages on their website, which they updated every half-hour as Bird moved through the countryside. They gave a description of the car, later broadcast its number plate, and released a photograph of the gunman, which they distributed to the media. As they monitored his progress they would urge the people of Whitehaven, Egremont, Seascale and lastly Boot to take shelter indoors.

On hearing this and receiving word that Bird had been sighted heading on the road towards Seascale, local Sam Edwards, 25, raised the alarm on the beach, urging the pleasure seekers who had gathered there to enjoy the half-term sunshine to run for cover.

Tragically, one person who was oblivious to this information was 23-year-old estate agent Jamie Clark, despite the efforts of Leanne Jarman, his fiancée, who was making desperate attempts to reach him on his mobile. 'I knew where Jamie was and tried to phone him but the signal was atrocious,' Leanne said. 'Everyone was trying to phone and no one could get through. I thought he would be okay. We didn't know Bird was heading that way.' But he was, and aiming straight into the path of the estate agent's Smart car. Clark had been driving back from a viewing when Bird shot at his vehicle, causing the younger man to crash and the car to overturn in the process. When the emergency services arrived at the scene, they assumed they were dealing with a road accident. They were shocked to discover that the driver had gunshot wounds.

It was 11.25am when Bird entered Seascale. Reaching a tunnel next to the station at Seascale, the cab-driver-turned-killer collided with a Land Rover. Harry Berger, a local pub landlord, had rushed into town to collect an important prescription for his wife. Reversing away from the vehicle Bird took aim at Berger. Realising that Bird was about to shoot at him, the publican instinctively raised his arm to his face. The gesture may have saved his life but his arm was badly wounded in the process. However, despite his injuries – the bullet was said to have taken away a part of Berger's arm – that seemed to be the last thing on his mind when Tony Whillock, who was passing by, rushed to help him. 'He was fully conscious, in shock,' said Whillock. 'But he gave me his wife's address and told me he had come into town to pick up an urgent prescription. I rang the pharmacy. It was extraordinary that he was thinking about his wife while in so much pain.'

William Hogg, a builder, heard the shots, as would David Moore, a reservist fire-fighter who had been pottering around in his garden at the time. He was to be called by his fire station to attend the scene of the crash and would help remove Berger from the Land Rover. According to Moore, Berger was in serious pain by now and was shouting out for help, which was 'distressing'. But they managed to remove the door of the car and get him to safety in a nearby café, which they transformed into a makeshift clinic. Berger would later be airlifted to hospital.

By this time Bird had escaped the scene – his car was captured on CCTV. Helicopters were circling the town and the police now had a location for him but having been just 30 seconds behind Bird as he entered Seascale, they suffered a further delay when they couldn't get past Berger's crashed Land Rover and were forced to wait until it was moved.

Just 26 seconds after Bird had shot at Harry Berger he would claim his next victim: 64-year-old Michael Pike, who was taking a morning bike ride along Drigg Road. Pike had also worked at Sellafield, where the murderer had once been employed. According to a nine-year-old boy, Jordan Williams, who – alarmingly given his age – witnessed the events as he walked by, Bird's taxi pulled up close behind the cyclist. 'He shot out his back tyre,' the boy said. 'As the cyclist was putting his foot down, the taxi stopped and the driver shot him in the cheek. There was blood everywhere. It was horrible.' Jordan had been with his sister Mia, aged four, another friend, and his mother Gill, who remembers seeing a grey-haired man in the car, who had 'piercing black eyes'. The mother and children had simply gone out to buy ice cream. 'It was terrifying,' Gill said. 'I keep thinking that if we had walked out of the door just a few seconds later, he might have shot us.'

Bird drove on and within just a couple of yards would encounter his final victim. Jane Robinson, a 66-year-old animal lover, was delivering catalogues along the street, not far from the house that she shared with her twin sister, Barrie. Once again Bird lured her to her death by called her over to his car and shooting her in the face.

Such was the extent of her injuries, not to mention those of Michael Pike, that when local GP Dr Barrie Walker arrived at the scene on the Drigg Road to help, he was horrified, saying that both bodies were beyond initial identification. 'I did not recognise the man on the bicycle but given his injuries that would not have been easy,' he said afterwards. 'Further up was another body. I thought it was a child at first, but it was a woman. She had catalogues in her hand. I had never seen shotgun injuries like this and people dying on the pavements in a quiet village... I have never seen anything like the ferocity of these injuries.'

As he drove on Bird would shoot again, blasting away at a woman walking up the hill in Seascale and later opening fire on a teenager. The police were just a matter of minutes behind him but, as CCTV footage would show, they were not able to close in on the killer in their 4x4 vehicles or their Volvo estate cars.

Bird drove out of Seascale, leaving scenes of both chaos and carnage in his wake, and headed east towards the tiny village of Boot and into the Lake District National Park. And it was there, in its beautiful surroundings, that Bird's spree came to an end.

The majority of the people out and about in the area were oblivious to the unfolding events of that morning. Whether they were families enjoying the half-term break, ramblers, or locals passing through, they had just gone out to enjoy the countryside and the weather. It wasn't until they heard the sound of helicopters overhead that they had the faintest idea that anything was wrong. The police were still unable to pinpoint Bird's precise location, but as part of a countywide containment plan they started blocking off roads and ushered villagers into their homes.

Speeding through the country lanes that surround the National Park, Bird encountered Nick James, who was holidaying in the area with his girlfriend Ruth. The couple had gone out for a drive and were travelling down a narrow country lane when they spotted Bird's Citroen coming in the opposite direction. They assumed that he would slow down and make way for them but, when it became clear that Bird was going to do nothing of the sort, James was forced to pull his car over instead, edging up to a stone wall. As Bird passed them he hit the wall on the other side, damaging his tyre in the process.

Nevertheless he continued on his journey and as he hurtled along he randomly took aim again. First at a campsite, which was filled with holidaymakers there on the half-term holiday, and at four other people, including a female walker and teacher Samantha Christie, shot while she was trying to take a photograph of the view. Both women would survive but they sustained serious injuries and had to be hospitalised.

The police were closing in on him now and had the parkland surrounded, but even if Bird had managed to find an escape route, his car was so badly damaged that he would crash on a quiet country lane, at the edge of woodland, just 400 yards from the point where he had tried to kill the walker, his final victim. Bird had lost a tyre as a result of his collision with the stone wall and the remaining ones were shredded.

Zoe and Lee Tucker, who were keen ramblers and who had come to the region with their sons for the half-term break, heard the noise of the crash. It was midday. Completely unaware of the trail of carnage Bird had left in his wake, the couple – with their sons Joshua, four, and Matthew, three, in tow – had come to see if they could help him, as an act of goodwill. They had seen his car weaving down the lane moments earlier and, judging by the scraping sound it was making on the road, they assumed that there was something wrong with the exhaust pipe.

But as they approached Bird, who was now out of the car and holding a gun across his chest, they immediately realised that something was wrong. Aside from the gun there was something sinister about the way he looked: he stared straight ahead vacantly, his eyes 'glassy'. Lee Tucker asked Bird what had happened and whether he was all right. Bird, monosyllabic, indicated that he had hit a stone. Coming towards them in the distance were two walkers who were signalling to Bird and the Tuckers that they had found the missing tyre and were gesturing to see whether he wanted it. Bird ignored them. Lee would try and communicate with him but he told him to 'just go'.

The murderer then looked Zoe, a 42-year-old chartered accountant from Buckinghamshire, straight in the eye and muttered: 'You're all right.' She had, of course, no notion of the significance of those three words, but both she and her husband were rightly concerned.

As Bird walked away – in what they would describe as an emotionless state with his shotgun in hand – over the humpback bridge that crossed the stream and disappeared into the woodland, 39-year-old Lee called 999. He felt uncomfortable with Bird's manner, the fact that he was armed, and also by the state of the car, which was littered with cartridges and a second gun, the rifle. Given that this was a rural community, Lee wasn't especially perturbed by the gun… it was the fact that there was a silencer attached that worried him. Ralph Jackson, a local man, whose farmhouse was just a quarter of a mile from the scene of the crash, was also deeply worried when he saw the abandoned vehicle. 'The window was smashed, there was a gun and it was filled with bullets and cartridges,' he said.

Disturbed by the encounter, the couple – who would be some of the last people to see Bird alive – made their way out of the parkland and towards the village of Boot. By now helicopters were circling overhead and the sound of police sirens rang through the air, shattering the tranquil silence of this beauty spot. When they approached the village of Boot and ran into three armed officers, they realised just what a lucky escape they'd had. They asked the police if they were looking for the 'man with the gun' and what he had done. When they were told that Derrick Bird had indiscriminately murdered numerous people, their hearts must have stopped.

At 1.30pm there was a shot heard from within the woodland. Bird had ended the rampage, and his life.

CHAPTER THREE

O n the morning of 2 June, Derrick Bird took the lives of twelve people during his murderous rampage. Some he knew: David Bird, Kevin Commons and Darren Rewcastle. The others: Susan Hughes, Isaac 'Spike' Dixon, Kenneth Fishburn, Jennifer and Jimmy Jackson, Gary Purdham, Jane Robinson, Jamie Clark and Michael Pike, he didn't. Needless to say, whether they were strangers or people familiar to him, they were all innocent victims and none of them deserved to have their lives cruelly taken away.

Their names would be gradually revealed one by one: a roll call of victims, each of whom had been brutally and violently murdered by the hand of Derrick Bird. But these folk were more than just 'victims', more than just names. Up until that fateful day in early June they had been people with a future ahead of them. Until Derrick Bird decided to play God and end their lives.

Whatever the reasons were for the rift between Derrick Bird and his twin David, according to the latter's three grown-up daughters he was a 'loving and cheerful' father and a devoted family man. In a statement released by his daughters Rachel, 28, Tracey, 26 and Katie, 19, the three girls spoke of their mutual devastation. 'He was the nicest man you could ever meet,' they said. 'He was a loving husband and doting dad and granddad. He will not only be missed by us, but by the whole community.' Although the 52-year-old had recently separated from his wife Susan, their split was said to be extremely amicable. He was well known across the area and enjoyed a good social life. People would speak of his 'kindness' and his 'humour'. And even though he had made a success of his various business ventures – enterprises associated with his skills as a mechanic and a building contractor – he was also said to be very 'laid back' and convivial.

There was an eccentric side to David. He would, at times, wear his overalls to bed, which was a long standing joke amongst family and friends, as was the fact that the successful businessman had never bothered to have a broken window repaired at the farmhouse. But unlike Derrick, who would suffer from bouts of paranoia at times, David had no objections to being teased by those close to him, in fact he would rather relish it, always willing to be the first to laugh at himself. Neighbours said David, who had recently been working as a lorry driver, was always at hand to help any of them out. He was very sociable, they would attest, and there was nothing that he liked more than meeting up with his friends and enjoying a drink or two, or having people round to his farmhouse, where he would entertain them with his jokes as he puffed away on his pipe.

Amongst David's many close friends was Kevin Commons, Bird's second victim. The 60-year-old solicitor was highly respected within his profession, a lawyer who believed in the power and the integrity of the British judicial system. Commons had set up a successful law firm – K J Commons – in the eighties, but was not interested in simply turning a profit. Instead, he saw it as his duty as a man of law to serve the entire community. He would keep his offices open not just for the individuals who could afford his services but also for impecunious folk who needed them. 'If anyone came through the door to ask for help he would help them, irrespective of whether they could pay,' said his business partner, Marcus Nickson. 'Nobody was ever turned away, and that was the principle on which he started the business. If somebody needed help, he was your man.'

Despite his charitable nature, Commons, who was married to his second wife Helen, could have afforded to retire. Not only was he successful as a solicitor – opening branches of his legal practice in Carlisle, Workington and Whitehaven but he was also a businessman. Nevertheless he believed his *raison d'être* was to continue helping others in his capacity as a lawyer. Kind and warm, he was also said to have held the respect of people within the community and the legal world. 'He was a staunch supporter of the criminal justice system absolutely in the fair treatment of everyone in the eyes of the law regardless of their means or background,' Nickson said. His friend, local businessman Gerard Richardson, said that Commons was not only 'One of the hardest-working people in the area,' but 'The single most generous person I've ever met. Certainly in his adversarial role you wouldn't want to cross him in the courtroom but [he was] just a really, lovely warm fellow.'

The third person on Bird's hit list of intended victims was a man known by many as 'The Chancer': Darren Rewcastle. The 43-year-old cab driver derived his nickname not only because he liked to gamble – he was reportedly a fan of playing slot machines – but also because he was a 'man of conviction', who would sometimes fearlessly stand up for things he felt passionate about. He was said to be something of a risk taker, a man who was not to immune to seeking out 'controversy'. He also loved just having a laugh, and had a wicked sense of humour.

'He was a real wind-up merchant,' a fellow driver from Whitehaven said of his former colleague. 'Always joking around. He was a top man.'

This 'loveable rogue' who was 'one of the lads' was a speedway and football fanatic, who had been especially looking forward to the World Cup in South Africa. Such was his passion for the game that he had recently staged a campaign to have the right to fly the England flag from his cab during the tournament, which had gained huge support from the locals. Tragically he wouldn't live to see the footballing event.

Rewcastle would be described as a 'star' by friends, and just days after his death over 600 messages of condolence would be left on his social networking website profile. Friends at the cab rank in Duke Street, Whitehaven, described him as cheerful and friendly, a person who liked to help others, raising huge amounts of money for charity. His parents were said to be 'heartbroken' at his death. Twice married and divorced he left behind a daughter, Savannah, aged 14.

Fellow cab drivers were bewildered as to why Bird would want to kill Rewcastle; even though they are said to have had a 'spat', the men were known to have been friends. They had even holidayed together and would often be spotted standing at the rank enjoying a chat together. In a tribute left to their son his parents wrote: 'To our darling son Darren. Sleep tight son, no one can hurt you now. We love and miss you so much. Nana will be looking after you now.'

Susan Hughes, 57, was the first of Bird's 'random' killings. The mother of two grown-up daughters, Susan was described as 'selfless' by her friends. Her youngest daughter Sarah, 27, is severely disabled and is said to be have been living in sheltered accommodation. She had lived with her mother until it simply became too much for Susan.

Susan Hughes, who lived in Egremont and worked part-time, devoted much of her days not only caring for Sarah, whom she visited every day, but also working in the local disability centre. Colleagues at the Copeland Occupational and Social Centre, in Cleator Moor, paid tribute to her, saying, 'Sue was so full of fun and a very important part of our caring team,' and, 'She was dedicated to her job.'

Ms Hughes, who was divorced, never made a fuss, despite her circumstances. She was said by friends to be 'quiet', 'self-effacing' and a 'dedicated' mother to both Sarah and her elder daughter Melinda, a social worker. She had been shopping for groceries when Bird shot her, and friends have said that amongst her supplies would have been treats for her beloved daughter Sarah.

Neighbour Alan Roberts recalled having friendly chats with her over the garden fence and spoke of how she would visit her daughter daily. He described her as being a woman, 'From the heart.' 'Not just in her work surroundings but in the home surroundings, round her family,' he added. In a statement read by the Chief Constable of Cumbria, Craig Mackey, her family described her as being a 'proud and determined mother', one who was 'completely irreplaceable to her family and her friends'.

At 71, Kenneth Fishburn was one of the oldest of Bird's victims, gunned down just 20 yards from his house. Fishburn had lived in Egremont for more than 20 years but he had travelled the world as a member of the armed forces and was a retired security guard at Sellafield. 'He was a lifetime army man, having served 25 years in the forces, serving with the Durham Light Infantry, which took him all over the world,' his family said of him in a statement. 'A further five years were served as a reservist, involving six months each year with the UN peacekeeping force.'

Mr Fishburn's neighbours said he was a 'thoroughly hard-working decent man.' He was well liked in the area and was enjoying his retirement. Each day he would take a long walk around the surrounding countryside, and would be seen stopping off at local cafes for a cup of tea or at the bookmakers, where he is said to have enjoyed the occasional 'flutter'. In a statement issued by his family they describe Fishburn as a 'quiet, private man' who 'liked nothing more than a few bets and game of snooker.'

Even though Kenneth Fishburn was a quiet man, locals say he was warm and kind and as a result had a wealth of friends and was a regular at the Egremont Conservative Club. Following his death the staff at the local branch of Ladbrokes laid out a wreath in his memory.

James and Jennifer Jackson, 67 and 68 respectively, were enjoying their retirement. They are described as 'a quiet, well mannered couple', who were both active in the local community.

Jennifer was a regular member of the congregation at her local church, and volunteered as their parish secretary. On the morning of her death she had been talking to the Rector of Egremont, discussing her sadness over the recent coach tragedy, in which two teenagers had lost their lives.

Moved as she was by what had happened, she told the Reverend Richard Lee to 'always look on the bright side of life.'

James, or 'Jimmy' as he was known to his friends, had spent his life working for the ambulance service. He was recovering from a recent operation on his gallbladder and was out taking a stroll that morning in order to get some air and take some gentle exercise. He had planned to meet up with his wife, who had popped out to buy a newspaper. The couple had two children, a son Christopher and a daughter Kathryn, both grown-up. Chris lived near them in the village. On a floral tribute left to the Jacksons by their goddaughter they were described as the 'loveliest of people'.

The Jacksons' family said the couple were 'wonderful, quiet, loving people right at the heart of the communities of Haile and Wilton'. Both were members of an over-sixties club and were heavily involved in village life.

To most of his friends Isaac Dixon was known as 'Spike' because of his tall, thin frame. The 65-year-old was a part-time mole catcher and dedicated countryman. According to his sister Margaret Earl he 'loved the outdoors and was very active'. He enjoyed going for walks with his dogs and, on the day he died, he had been out in the countryside working alongside a local farmer.

Like many locals, he too had worked at Sellafield, but had been forced to retire early due to health reasons. He was divorced but was in a loving relationship with his girlfriend

Pat. The father-of-two and grandfather-of-six was known to be a fine citizen, always happy to help his elderly neighbours, doing odd jobs for them regularly such as giving them fresh eggs from his hens. 'He'd help anyone who asked him,' his brother Tom Dixon said.

Isaac Dixon's neighbour, Joan Ferguson, agreed, saying: 'He helped everybody, he was that sort of person. He was a gentleman. He did a lot for everybody if anybody wanted him. He will be sadly missed.' Only recently, Dixon had helped arrange a charity evening with a country-and-western theme at the Egremont Conservative Club, raising £1000 for the charity Help for Heroes.

Thanks to his sporting prowess, Gary Purdham was something of a local hero. The former rugby player had played at a semi-professional level for Whitehaven and Workington – his younger brother, Rob, currently captains Harlequins, one of the top teams in the country. Purdham was only 31 years old, and father to two young children. Friends have spoken about his sense of humour and team-mates from the clubs he played for were quick to come forward to pay their respects to him.

David Bowden, chairman of Workington Town rugby league club said, 'He was quite simply a gentleman and a real pleasure to know. He had a wonderful calm and mature temperament. As a result, he was one of those players that his team-mates looked up to.'

Purdham was a local lad through and through; his family have farmed in the area for many years. On the day that he encountered Bird, he was cutting hedgerows on the land. He was happily married to wife Ros, and lived with her and their two young sons, aged two and eight, in Beckerment. At the first Whitehaven Rugby Club home match following the shootings, Ros released 12 white doves on the pitch before the game in commemoration of her husband and to the other lives that were lost that day.

The youngest of Bird's victims was just 23 years old. Jamie Clark, an estate agent, died when his Smart car came into the killer's path in Seascale. Clark, who was working with the lettings team at the Belvoir estate agency in Cockermouth, had moved to the area from Buckinghamshire in 2008 when he became engaged to his fiancée Leanne Jarman, who had come to Carlisle to study. Colleague Ryan Park said that Clark was one of the 'nicest lads' he had ever met. 'He never said a bad word about anyone,' he recalled. 'We're absolutely gutted to have lost him.'

Clark was the son of a National Lottery millionaire. His family's lives had changed forever in 2001 when his parents Richard and Jane Clark won £2.3 million. As his brother John would explain, one minute their lives were 'perfect' and they couldn't be happier, the next – thanks to the actions of Derrick Bird – 'it's just worthless'. 'Our lives will never be the same again,' his parents said in a statement. 'He was the most wonderful, gentle, loving, considerate man.'

Leanne, who planned to marry Clark in 2012, said: 'He was not just my fiancé, but my closest friend. He is my life. My world, my everything. Taken too soon, he gave so many people love and joy. He touched so many lives but he did not know how cherished he was.'

Michael Pike, a devoted husband, father and grandfather, had retired to Cumbria in order to enjoy the simple pleasures in life with his wife Sheena. The 64-year-old was taking his daily bike ride and was just a stone's throw from his home in Seascale when Bird shot him.

As well as riding his bike, walking in the fells and exploring the Lake District, Pike had a keen interest in politics and current affairs. It was something that would come in useful during his time at Sellafield, where he was appointed a trade union organiser. Jude Talbot, his daughter, said he loved to dote on his three grandchildren, and was well respected within the community. By all accounts he was a man who loved to make the most out of life.

In addition to following his many interests Pike had taken an Open University degree at the age of 40. 'He loved living here,' Jude said. 'It was his idea of paradise.' She also spoke of his wit and joviality: 'At times he made us laugh until our tummies hurt. He had a great sense of humour and a great sense of fun.'

At the time of his death Michael Pike was enjoying life, according to his family, who also said: '[He] was happier at this time than at any time before. He loved this area and spent much of his time walking and cycling locally. It was sad that his enjoyment of his well-earned leisure was cut short. But he will always be remembered as the man he was, and for the things he did in his life. He died a contented man and we are proud of him.'

The last of Bird's victims was Jane Robinson, a 66-year-old animal lover, who was killed as she set about doing her part-time job of delivering catalogues for the storage company Betterware. Bird would shoot Ms Robinson yards away from the home she shared with her twin sister, Barrie, in Seascale.

She was known locally as the 'pigeon woman', an affectionate nickname given to her as a result of her passion for the birds, which she kept as pets and was 'especially fond of'. She and Barrie, neither of whom had married, would often be seen out feeding the pigeons in Seascale and in 1998 the sisters were featured on ITV, campaigning to save birds contaminated by radioactivity from Sellafield. She worked tirelessly for the registered charity PDSA and later devoted more of her time to caring for birds.

Jane Robinson, who is described as a 'real Seascale person', was an active member of the community and a regular churchgoer. Although she and Barrie were said to be private people, they were always prepared to help their neighbours, often doing gardening for them.

'Whenever anyone was ill she would take flowers for them,' William Hogg, a lifelong friend of the sisters said. 'She was just a very nice lady.' According to Jordan Williams, the nine-year-old who had witnessed the murder of Michael Pike, she was a 'nice woman'. 'She used to tell me to watch out for adders in the grass at the bottom of the garden,' he remembered. 'She died. It's very sad.'

Her death has left her sister, to whom she was exceptionally close, devastated. 'She was the best sister I could ever have and as twins we were especially close,' Barrie Robinson commented. 'Her kindness to people extended to animals and birds. She was caring, considerate and generous.'

Twelve innocent people, whose lives were tragically and violently cut short on the whim of just one man. Their killer and the date of their deaths inextricably bind their names together forever.

There was the jovial mechanic who was a dedicated family man; the lawyer prepared to help anyone in the community, regardless of whether they could afford it or not; the humorous and much-loved cab driver described as being 'one of a kind'; the mother of two who had devoted her life to caring for the disabled; the retired soldier who had worked as a peacemaker; the respected member of the local parish, who worked tirelessly for her church – and her husband, who had dedicated his entire adult life working for the ambulance service; the countryman and part-time mole catcher who cared for the elderly and raised money for charity.

Add to the list the immensely popular and respected sportsman – father of two young children; the kind, charming and affable estate agent about to embark on a new chapter of his life with his fiancée; the country-loving family man who lived life to the full and was enjoying his retirement; and, finally, the gentle animal lover, who worked tirelessly for the community.

Their ages may be wide-ranging, but these were people who had a lot to live for. They were community spirited, working for the good of others, and they looked out not only for the people they knew but even for the ones they didn't. Colourful, caring, loving, loyal and warm, these were people who loved West Cumbria, individuals who were intent on giving something back. They were sons and daughters, brothers and sisters, fathers and mothers and grandparents. People who were much loved by family, friends and colleagues, as the multitude of heartfelt tributes paid to them in the ensuing days would attest.

They were public-spirited people who had worked hard for all they had achieved and didn't expect anything more from life; they only wanted to give something back. They enjoyed simple, uncomplicated lives, whether it was walking the land, gardening and farming, caring for animals, supporting football, working for the church, cycling, following current affairs, simply being with their partners or their families, or looking after the elderly and the disabled. People who were proud to call themselves Cumbrians.

CHAPTER FOUR

As news broke that Derrick Bird had ended his deadly rampage by taking his own life in the woodland of the Lake District National Park, the people of West Cumbria, who had only hours before had been told to seek refuge indoors by the police, slowly began to emerge from their homes and gather at central points in their hamlets, villages and towns. Shocked, bewildered and visibly upset they stood together in silence trying to make sense of the events of that morning, trying to comprehend the fact that within just a couple of hours they had lost so many of their loved ones.

Had this happened in a more urban environment maybe people would have stayed indoors, too frightened to walk out on the streets. But Derrick Bird didn't commit his crime in an inner city. Instead he carried out his rampage in

West Cumbria, a place where community means everything to the people who live there. They didn't want to mourn alone, to shut themselves away. Their natural instinct was to come together and share their collective sense of shock, bewilderment and grief with one another. They wanted to be there for one another, and stand side by side.

In the hours that followed the spree impromptu shrines began to appear all over the 45-mile radius where Bird had carried out his brutal killings. Floral tributes were laid, candles were lit, and hand-crafted crosses marked the spots where loved ones had fallen.

It is has been said that since the death of the Princess of Wales in 1997 and the unprecedented outpouring of public grief that subsequently followed, the people of Britain have learned to grieve in a more public, less introverted, way. And looking at the many tributes that had been left around Whitehaven and Seascale alone it is difficult not to reflect on those scenes outside Kensington Palace in the days that followed her death: the candles, the toys, the handwritten cards, the sea of bouquets that had been left in her memory.

But the difference here is that the tributes left for the victims of Derrick Bird aren't from strangers, they had not been left by people who believed they somehow 'knew' the deceased. They did actually know him. They were left by parents, children, colleagues from work, friends and neighbours. The teddies were left by grandchildren and nephews and nieces, the beautiful hand-crafted cards put there by godchildren and neighbours. There was nothing mawkish about any of it – the gestures were heartfelt, personal and poignant... like the teddy bear and toy digger left at David Bird's farmhouse, laid by his grandchildren. There was a beautifully decorated board in Wilton, which paid tribute to the Jacksons, a wreath left outside Ladbrokes for Kenneth Fishburn, and a Workington and Whitehaven rugby scarf tied to a post where Gary Purdham fell. Each of these tributes would serve only to affirm the incredible closeness of this community.

Within hours of the story of the rampage breaking on the national news, the media descended on West Cumbria. Helicopters trying to catch aerial shots of the parkland where Derrick Bird spent his final hours whirred overhead. Satellite vans lined the streets leading into Whitehaven and Seascale. Reporters giving live-to-studio reports dotted the streets, newspaper journalists, photographers and cameramen were all out in force. If the people of West Cumbria found it intrusive, being ever dignified and warm, they didn't voice their anger or frustration but simply accepted the attention. As one local said: 'It's to be expected and if getting the story out there stops this from happening again then so be it.' Accordingly, many of them would assist the media in their work, giving interviews on what they had witnessed that day, and giving testimonials on the character of Derrick Bird, and tributes to the people they had lost.

The story of what happened on the morning of 2 June would preoccupy most of the national news that evening, with some television and radio stations extending their programmes as a result. And it wasn't just of national interest either, for it would be followed up by news crews and publications across the world.

In the House of Commons that afternoon the mood was sombre. This being Prime Minister's Question Time, and the first such session since the coalition government had been formed, by rights it should have been a rowdy affair. But by 2.30pm, as they gathered in the chamber, the majority of the MPs had heard the news. So they sat in total silence as they waited for the proceedings to begin.

And as they did so the police began their arduous task of launching their investigations. Over the 45-mile radius in which Bird had carried out his spree there would be over 30 crime scenes. The landscape of West Cumbria was punctuated with police vans, cordoning tape, small white tents, and a battalion of forensic investigators. In Rowrah officers would arrive at Derrick Bird's modest home and would sift through his possessions bit-by-bit in an attempt to find both evidence and clues as to why he had committed the atrocities. Correspondence was removed from his house, as was his computer and boxes of ammunition. Officers on the ground would interview neighbours and friends, whilst in the Lake District National Park they would carefully move his abandoned car so that it could be examined in a controlled environment.

That evening the Queen expressed her 'heartfelt sympathy' to the grieving. 'I was deeply shocked by the appalling news from Cumbria,' she said in her tribute. 'In asking you to pass my deepest and most heartfelt sympathy to the families of all those who were killed and to the injured themselves, I am sure that I share the grief and horror of the whole country.' Pope Benedict XVI would also send a message of condolence to the families touched by the tragedy. In a statement from the Vatican, which was only made public later on, the Pope asked for 'forgiveness, hope and reconciling love' as the people of West Cumbria came to terms with their loss. The statement continued: 'His Holiness Pope Benedict XVI asks you kindly to convey the assurance of his spiritual closeness to all who have been affected by the recent tragic events in West Cumbria.'

Prime Minister David Cameron would echo these sentiments, while on the social networking site Facebook more than 11,000 mourners would pay their respects to those affected as they joined the group 'RIP To The Victims of Derrick Bird'. Locally, the Reverend John Bannister, of Whitehaven, would pay tribute to his community noting that the whole 'appalling episode' had been 'out of character' for the region, saying: 'The whole of West Cumbria is in a complete spirit of disbelief.'

Jamie Reed, the MP for Copeland, said that while locals had been shocked by the events they would also come together and try and pull through it. 'It's an incredibly close-knit community, it's one of our great strengths,' the MP said in an interview with GMTV. 'If you hurt one of us you hurt all of us, that is the way we are. We will be doing everything we can now as a community, coming together to help the families of the victims, to help everyone that has been affected by this. That is our priority.' In the ensuing days the National Health Service, the Samaritans and other support groups would offer counselling to the people of West Cumbria – whether it was to the victims themselves, the bereaved, those who had witnessed the shootings, or simply to those who felt touched by the episode. Their pledge was to be on hand for them.

At the West Cumberland Hospital in Whitehaven, and the Cumberland Infirmary in Carlisle, medical teams worked twenty-four-seven to care for the injured. Some of the 24 who had been shot that morning were able to be discharged that day, whilst others were in a more serious condition. The staff would treat and care for the wounded with professional aplomb, but most had never seen anything like it. Charles Brett, a consultant at the West Cumberland, admitted that they had not previously had to deal with any such situation. Just ten days before, his team had been on hand to treat the teenagers who had been injured in the terrible coach crash. Now they were trying to cope with this. Gunshot wounds to the head were 'uncommon' in this part of the country he admitted, but nevertheless the medical professionals rallied together and Charles Brett would heap praise on his team, two of whom had previously spent time treating combat victims in Iraq.

When the Prince of Wales came to Cumbria the following week he had nothing but high praise for the medical teams who'd dealt with the aftermath of the shootings. He spent many hours talking to doctors and nurses at the West Cumberland Hospital as well spending time with the survivors. Dr Michael Green, a hospital consultant, said the visit from Prince Charles had given both patients and staff a morale boost, especially to those working in the Accident and Emergency Department, who had to deal with two tragic incidents within the space of ten days. 'His visit helps us to understand that the nation has been affected by these events, and that people want to support and help us through these difficult days,' he said afterwards.

The Prince of Wales, who said he was 'utterly devastated by the killings', sent his sympathy to all involved in 'these brutally tragic circumstances'. He also met the rector of Whitehaven and minsters from other faiths, and community and civic leaders at St Nicholas's Church in the town. There he would add his name to the book of condolence, signing simply: 'In deepest sympathy, Charles'.

The prince also spent time that day meeting some of the bereaved families, including David Bird's widow Susan and their three daughters, Rachel, Tracey and Katie. 'Prince Charles spent time with Susan and the girls and his heart went out to them,' their local vicar said. 'He was very understanding of the pain they are going through and that lifted them a bit. They left the meeting with a little bit of a spring in their step.'

David Cameron also visited the area. This would be the first national tragedy that Cameron would have to deal with since becoming Prime Minister, just weeks earlier. Mr Cameron had already given a press conference at Downing Street two days after the shootings, in which he promised that the government would do everything they possibly could to prevent such a crime ever happening again. 'We must do absolutely everything to complete this investigation, to make sure that everything is done to make sure that events like this cannot happen again in our country and to bring these communities back together,' he pledged at the time.

When asked whether that meant toughening up Britain's gun laws, the Prime Minister said it was too soon to jump to conclusions, and that it was important to wait until a full investigation had been completed. Warning against any 'knee-jerk reactions' he said markedly: 'You can't legislate to stop a switch flicking in someone's head.'

Two days later Mr Cameron and the new Home Secretary, Theresa May, travelled to Cumbria and spent two hours talking to the survivors who'd been injured in the attack. Both praised their bravery. They would also meet with members of the emergency services – the police, ambulance crews and medical teams who had been on duty that day, as well as members of the Civil Nuclear Police, in charge of guarding Britain's nuclear sites, including Sellafield.

The Prime Minister later held a meeting at the Workington Police Station with Cumbria's Chief Constable, Craig Mackey, and his team of investigating officers and detectives, and was given a progress report. 'Obviously, people here in West Cumbria have suffered the most appalling tragedy and it will have a huge impact on the community,' Mr Cameron said after the visit. 'I wanted to come here to show that the government wanted to listen, wanted to show how much it cares about what has happened here. Some of the people I have met here are having to come to terms with the most appalling random acts that they will find very difficult to understand – and in some cases there will be no proper explanation.

'There will be some parts of this that we will never understand,' he continued. 'There will be some random acts of killing, and people who will have lost loved ones will ask why it happened to them and why it was so random: why it is so unfair and cruel, what's happened here. There are some incredible stories of bravery and an amazing community has been torn apart by this, but they will eventually come through like other communities have.'

Whether this process would take a matter of years, or decades, possibly even longer, one can't say, but what the people of West Cumbria demonstrated during those first few days after the events of 2 June is that they are a community who will deal with this tragedy together, side-by-side. And just four days after the episode they would do this, quite literally, as they congregated that Sunday at services all over the region to remember their loved ones.

More than a 1000 people gathered in the gardens of St Nicholas's Church in Whitehaven for a service of remembrance and recollection, and in Seascale, where the service was held on the beach, they came in droves.

Despite the wind and the rain that had bucketed down throughout the day both services were held in the open air, as organisers knew that they would never fit everyone into their places of worship and they said they didn't want to hold either remembrance service behind closed doors.

Instead people sat huddled together under umbrellas in their waterproofs as, together, they sang hymns, listened to readings and prayed for their loved ones. The young and the elderly alike braved the weather for the hour-long services, for nothing was going to stop them from paying their respects. Children perched on their parents' shoulders, and laid flowers at the end of the services; war veterans wiped tears from their eyes; mothers brought babies and toddlers along in their pushchairs. Police and fire-fighters stood alongside local dignitaries. They sang hymns, listened to the eulogies and the readings, and prayed for their loved ones. And as the names of the twelve victims were read out one-by-one, the silence was palpable.

Addressing the congregation at the service in Whitehaven, where messages of sympathy from the Queen and Prince Charles were read out by the Lord Lieutenant of Cumbria, the Bishop praised the spirit of the West Cumbrian people, describing them as 'tough as teak, gentle as a lamb'. He said: 'The sharing of each other's burden will be crucial to the healing of each other's communities over the long run.'

Meanwhile in Seascale the Reverend Richard Teale, chairman of the Cumbrian Methodist District, said, referring to the sense of the community: 'Perhaps we are a more loving people, more sensitive, more concerned for each other because of the tragic events of these last few days.' Teale noted that everyone in the town would have known at least one person who had been killed. 'Someone once said that tragedy does not take love away – it actually increases it,' he added. Following the Seascale service people were invited to lay single flowers at the foot of a simple cross which had been made from driftwood.

Smaller, more personal services would be held around the area – at the Haile Parish Church where the Jacksons worshipped, for example. One week later the community of West Cumbria would come together again for further services of remembrance, this time meeting at seven separate locations across the towns and villages where the killings took place. The services were held simultaneously, starting at 11.45am and ending just before the strike of noon, when a minute's silence was observed. Across the country people would follow suit – from the Houses of Parliament to offices and schools. And when in Whitehaven the minute came to an end, the cab drivers of Duke Street, standing upright next to their cars, would sound their horns together, in a final salute to the ones they had loved and lost.

CHAPTER FIVE

The people of West Cumbria, united in their grief and suffering, may have pledged to stand side by side with one another as they came to terms with their sorrow, but for one family within that community things wouldn't be so straightforward. The events of 2 June would leave this family, once very much at the epicentre of West Cumbrian life, feeling isolated, removed and out on their own. And rather than being 'distressed', 'heartbroken' or even angry about what had happened, instead they would be left feeling 'shocked', 'dismayed', even 'mortified'. These people were, of course, the family of Derrick Bird himself.

For his sons Graeme and Jamie, for his elder surviving brother Brian and Brian's wife Susan, for Linda Mills, who had given Derrick his children, and for Mary Bird, the gunman's frail and elderly mother, it was almost impossible to even start to comprehend how it had apparently come to this. Could this man, this person now being called a mass murderer across the media, really be the same person they had known and loved?

It would be left to the Reverend Jim Marshall, a local curate who has lived in the area for 23-years and who knew the Birds well, to best articulate what the family were going through at the time. 'There was the Derrick they knew for 52 years,' he said. 'And then there was a new Derrick for a few hours last Wednesday. They can make no sense at all of what was behind it.'

Standing outside St Michael's Church in Lamplugh, the curate read statements from Derrick's sons and on behalf of his brother Brian, who until that moment on Sunday the sixth of June had yet to make any comment on the episode. 'They have wanted to make a statement for quite a while,' the curate explained as the press gathered. 'And they have wanted that to be made in truth and honesty.'

The statement from Graeme and Jamie read: 'To us, he was nicest man you could ever meet. He was a loving dad and recently had become a grandfather. We would like to say that we do not know why our dad committed these horrific crimes. We are both mortified by these sad events.

'Dad was a loving and cheerful character and was well known throughout the local community and in the areas where he worked. He will be missed by us, his family and friends. We would also like to send our condolences to all the other families and people involved in this tragic incident. Our thoughts are with them.'

Graeme and Jamie would ask to be able to mourn their father privately.

In a separate statement written by Brian he said that both he and his family were 'extremely saddened' and that the loss of both his younger brothers, who were 'very caring, family people', was 'devastating'. And just as his nephews had, Brian also extended his condolences to those that had been injured in the shootings, and those who had been bereaved. 'We appreciate that they are suffering at this time,' his statement went on. 'We cannot offer any reason why Derrick took it upon himself to commit these crimes. We are in shock and dismay.'

There would be no statement from Mary Bird for by then the 87-year-old, who had been suffering from cancer and was also recovering from a stroke, had been readmitted to hospital.

Stunned by what had happened, confused about what had motivated him to do it, grieving the loss of Derrick Bird, his family retreated back into their own worlds as they came to terms with it all. Graeme and Victoria closed the curtains of their house in Lamplugh and for a time decamped to the latter's mother's house with their baby. Jamie, in the middle of his GCSE exams, remained at home with Linda in Lamplugh: a police officer was placed outside her door. And Brian tried to carry on as best he could – caring for his mother and trying to keep his family together.

History doesn't relate how Graeme and Jamie learnt of their father's actions and subsequent suicide but, according to Rev Marshall, Brian first realised what was going on when a neighbour knocked on his door just before 1pm. She steered him away from the house and told him of what was unfolding. In the meantime Mary, who was staying with Brian and Susan at the time, went to turn on the lunchtime television news – as she always did at this time of day while Susan prepared a meal in the kitchen.

By the time Brian came back into the house Mary already had the television on. 'The first thing that came on was the horrible news,' the curate said. 'That was the first moment the family knew of it. [Mary] was horrified. For an old lady that age, with two sons now dead, that's dreadful enough. But to realise that one of her sons has caused so much chaos in the lives of so many others, that's what is hurting her more than anything else.'

Seeing the news initially made Brian and Susan terrified for their own lives. 'If you realised that your brother had killed his twin… it was all a shock. They had a 52-year-old brother, son, husband and father, and he had killed his own twin brother. And they heard he had been killing other people. What would you do?' Marshall asked.

Without a moment's hesitation the couple locked all the doors and windows of their property before Brian called the police, who told him to stay put. Three quarters of an hour later they called him back to tell him that it was 'over' and that Derrick had taken his own life.

According to Marshall the couple were in a state of shock, as was Mary. The following day she would be readmitted to hospital.

In the days that followed the family would try and make sense of what had happened but despite lengthy conversations between them all, no one could offer an answer. As far as they were concerned there was no 'open family rift' or 'feud'. They were unaware, as reports would have it, that Derrick was being investigated for tax fraud − it was 'news' to them. 'There's no explanation for why he flipped, and that's what he's done, he's flipped,' Marshall explained.

Even though Mary had watched the events unfolding on the news friends say that having been hospitalised the following day for a time she was unaware of the full extent of what her younger son had perpetrated, and that in the days that followed she had serious difficulties in coming to terms with what had happened. Back at Cockermouth Hospital she kept asking to see her sons. Her cousin Joy Ryan said the full impact of the tragedy 'just wouldn't sink in'. 'She kept saying she wanted to talk to them − she wanted to talk to her sons,' Joy said. In another conversation with Rev Marshall she told the curate: 'I don't know what's happened. It's so awful. I can't explain it.'

'She was horrified,' Rev Marshall said. 'She was astounded.'

In view of the delicate situation, the family decided in those first few days not to reveal the full extent of Derrick's crimes to Mary Bird all at once, for they knew it would be too much for her to bear. It would be over a week before her daughter-in-law gently broke the whole story to her. For the poor lady, losing two sons, her twins, at once was a tragedy in itself. But to know that one of the pair had been killed by the hand of the other was incomprehensible to her.

Friends say that Mary and Derrick had always been close. Rev Marshall, who had seen Bird at his mother's bedside when she was in hospital the month before, had described him as a 'splendid' and a very 'personable person', and was of the opinion that he was devoted to his mother. 'Derrick used to go round his mum's for his tea. He felt he was giving her a purpose,' the curate added. 'He was a caring man.'

A neighbour in Rowrah confirmed the fact of Derrick's close relationship with his mother, saying that he would visit her every day at teatime. 'He was devoted to his mother. He said he liked to make sure she was all right and he'd been worried about her health recently because she had been so poorly,' they said. 'You couldn't fault him as a son. He was just wonderful to her.'

That her 'loving' and 'caring' son would murder her other child, his own twin, was of course a completely alien concept to Mary Bird. And then there were his other victims; the lives he had ruined and torn apart. For someone like Mary, a churchgoer and a woman dedicated to her community, it was a heavy cross to bear.

For Graeme and Jamie it was difficult too. They had lost a much-loved father. The boys may not have lived with him but he was very much part of their lives, and friends say that he was a good father to both of them. 'He was proud of his lads,' a neighbour said. 'Very proud. He was happy when Graeme got married and talked about the wedding a lot and then was chuffed to bits when he became a grandfather. He was beaming. And he loved being with Jamie. He looked forward to seeing him and doing things with him, like taking him diving.'

In their statement Graeme and Jamie had described their father as 'cheerful' and 'loving' but now they would have to also somehow acknowledge, to themselves at least, that the parent they had loved so much throughout their lives had killed in cold blood.

And then there was Brian. The 58-year-old had just lost both his brothers and would mourn their loss. But as he dealt with his own grieving process he would also resolutely aim to keep his family together: caring for Mary, whilst trying to maintain the bond between his brothers' families. He would step into the breach arranging a painful first meeting where they all got together. He would help to organise the funerals of the two men, discussing the possibility of whether the brothers who had been born together should be buried that way – an idea that was later to be dismissed by all.

And yet while all of this was going on he must have kept asking himself why it had come to this. The family have denied that there were any family feuds, have denied any knowledge of personal or legal disputes between Derrick and David, and yet there must have been moments following the shootings when Brian Bird wondered whether he had missed anything.

As Rev Marshall said in a statement of his own: 'The family put no blame on Derrick. They knew Derrick for 52 years. There was a new Derrick for a few hours last Wednesday, and the two things are very separate in the eyes of members of the family.'

When Mary Bird learnt of the full extent of the carnage her younger son had wreaked across West Cumbria, despite her weakened state she asked to see Rev Marshall while in her hospital bed. 'I asked her how things were and she said she had been thinking it over and asked me to help compose letters to every one of the families who were bereaved. She is very determined like that,' he said. 'She does not know how to deal with it,' he added. 'Though I am sure writing letters will be part of her understanding and healing process. She says, "I just can't take it in, Jim. I don't know how it happened".'

Rev Marshall said the rest of the family felt the same. 'If they had the strength, they are the sort of people who would have gone round to each member of the families of those people who had been shot, killed and wounded, in order to apologise for what has happened. Having said that, their brother, father and son is a person who in all sorts of respects still has their respect, because he was not the person that they saw and heard about on Wednesday. For 52 years they knew one man. For several hours they heard about another.'

CHAPTER SIX

So what was it that led Derrick Bird, an ostensibly mild mannered and affable character, with family, friends and a network of neighbours and colleagues to suddenly turn and commit such a violent crime against his own people? His family have said that it was completely out of character, his colleagues were left dumbfounded by it, as were his neighbours. Indeed, not a single person who knew Derrick Bird seemed to believe that he was capable of such an act. 'Nice', 'kind', 'quiet' was how they described him and even those who said that Bird could be moody at times were finding it hard to comprehend that such a temperament would lead him to kill. As far as they were concerned 'Birdy' was just an ordinary man, living an ordinary life.

It is interesting to note that in the weeks following the killings few people who knew Bird had a bad word to say about him. For all the destruction he caused, the hurt and the loss, they still refused to condemn him. Even the ones he shot at had trouble seeing him as anything other than the man he was before the second of June. Paul Williams, the cab driver Bird tried to shoot in the face, would only say that he was 'a really nice man'. 'He isn't at all aggressive.' Williams asserted. 'He's a good guy.' Maybe it was shock that would lead the near-victim to keep talking about Bird in the present tense, maybe he thought in doing so he would be able to keep alive the spirit of the man he had known and liked prior to that terrible day. Maybe it was easier that way.

But Williams wasn't alone in wanting to remember Derrick Bird for who was before, rather than confront the reality of who he had become. For whatever reason, none of them could begin to even allow themselves to think of Bird as a monster. In their eyes, as Rev Jim Marshall said, there seemed to be two Derrick Birds. The one they had known and loved for many years, and the one that went on the rampage that morning, intent on taking the lives of so many innocent people.

If this was the case then, what was it that caused such a dramatic change in Derrick Bird? How and why could someone turn from being a loving family man, friend and neighbour into a merciless killer, seemingly overnight? David Cameron had described it as a 'switch that flicks in someone's head'. Is that what happened to Derrick Bird?

In the absence of a suicide note and with the one man who knew the answer to the mystery now dead, family and friends, plus the people he injured and left bereaved could spend a lifetime speculating on this.

As Deputy Chief Constable Stuart Hyde, of the Cumbrian Police, would state in a conference: 'It may well be that we never actually find what caused this.' Nevertheless, just hours after the killings the investigation would begin in earnest, with every aspect of Derrick Bird's life delved into. No stone would be left unturned. 'We are looking at Derrick Bird's financial aspects, his relationships with his family and those with his colleagues, a whole menu to help piece together why it happened,' Hyde explained in a press conference.

The police, like the rest of West Cumbria, would need to fathom what caused such a seemingly nice and ordinary man to suddenly morph into a brutal killer. They needed to discover who or what it was that caused the 'switch to flick' in the mind of Derrick Bird.

In the run-up to the killings many of the people who knew well him say that they hadn't noticed anything different about Bird. By all accounts he had enjoyed his weekend and on Sunday, together with his brothers, he had visited his mother for tea, where, according to Rev Marshall, they had enjoyed a pleasant afternoon.

On Monday there had been the trip to Bassenthwaite Lake to watch his son compete in the Motocross trials. He had been on good form that day and had enjoyed the weather.

'He was sitting under an awning with his friends and having a laugh,' reported Peter Foley, landlord of The Hound in Frizington. 'You would never have thought there was anything wrong.'

Two neighbours who saw him returning home that day said he seemed to be his usual, cheery self, waving to them as he passed them by.

Later that evening Bird popped into The Hound for a drink with some friends. According Michelle Haigh, Foley's partner, Bird was 'his usual self'. He'd usually have two or three pints and a bit of a gossip with people and then go home,' she said. 'That's what he did on Monday – he was just normal Derrick.' The landlord said that Bird was one of last people to leave at closing time, continuing: 'It was just usual "Good night Derrick" and off he went, as he always did. He was just a normal, sociable bloke.'

On Tuesday 1 June, the eve of the killings, he had visited Graeme and Victoria at their house in a quiet cul-de-sac in Cleator Moor, which is just a four-mile drive from Rowrah. He visited the couple because he wanted to make his grandson a financial gift, and during that meeting he asked to hold baby Leighton in his arms. That afternoon he also visited a friend, Gary Kennett, from the Solway diving club, to whom he gave some diving equipment. A neighbour recalled seeing him sitting on his doorstep drinking a cup of tea in the sun. 'I said hello and he said hello back. There wasn't any sign of a problem,' they said.

But at some point during the latter part of that day Bird's mood would darken. Another neighbour who encountered him in Rowrah in the late afternoon said he 'wasn't himself'. They had greeted him on the street expecting him to wave back or exchange a few words but Bird didn't even acknowledge them, which they claim was distinctly out of character. Instead he seemed to look right through them and walked on by.

It was clear by now that something was preying on his mind. Visiting the cab rank in Whitehaven in the early hours of the evening he seemed troubled and agitated. When driver Mark Cooper, a man whom he knew and trusted well, asked him what the matter was, Bird told him that he was worried that 'he was going down for four years'.

Bird was alluding to the fact that he was being investigated for tax evasion by the Inland Revenue for the sum of £60,000, which the police have since confirmed. It appears that the self-employed cab driver had not been declaring his full income and was now facing a demand for several years of unpaid taxes. Friends say Bird not only lacked the funds to pay off the debt but also feared that he would be imprisoned for tax evasion.

A family friend confirmed this, saying: 'I was told he hadn't paid any taxes for a long time and was worried that the authorities were about to catch up with him. People are saying he owed a lot of money,' the friend said. Given the fact that Bird was receiving his fares in cash this would have been easy for him to do, and apparently he had not only been doing this for years but in that time had squirreled away vast sums of money, hoarding it under the floorboards of his house in Rowrah where, according to one friend, there 'must have been thousands of pounds in ten-pound notes'. He was said to have been anxious that soon the notes would no longer be legal tender, referring to the fact that the £20 note featuring the head of Edward Elgar was to be withdrawn in June.

Mark Cooper wasn't the only friend that Bird confided in about his tax problems. Bob Cullen, another driver and fellow member of the Solway Sub-Aqua Club, who had been Bird's diving partner for 12 years, said that Derrick had told him of his financial problems when they were holidaying in Croatia back in September 2009.

'We were in Croatia when he started telling me about his money troubles,' Cooper said. 'He kept it under wraps until he got drunk. Essentially he wasn't declaring his earnings and hadn't paid any tax. If he made £150 he told the accountant he had made £20 and pocketed the rest. His house was full of cash. He didn't use banks, he put it under the floorboards and inside the mattress. Years ago he lifted the floorboards and discovered that he had £10,000-worth of old £10 notes. The notes had changed but he hadn't realised.' According to Mark Cooper, the tax issue had been going on for the past six months, although he'd only shared this information with him a couple of weeks before. Bird was 'terrified' by the prospect of going to prison and 'kept worrying about it'. 'All he said was that they had caught him with £60,000 in the bank.'

Bird was so worried that he confided in another driver

who had once served time. He wanted to know what prison was like, because he was convinced he was going to be sent down. The driver told him that he thought it was unlikely but his assurances fell on deaf ears.

The tax issue was clearly hanging over Bird's head that evening, for it would come up in conversation again that night when he visited the house of Neil Jacques and his wife Carol. He spent six hours there. Jacques, a 52-year-old car mechanic, was an old friend of Bird's, a neighbour in Rowrah, and the two men occupied the evening talking before watching *On Deadly Ground*, a violent action movie starring Steven Segal. No alcohol was consumed that night; instead the men spent the evening simply drinking coffee.

'He had something on his mind – that he was going to jail for tax evasion,' Jacques said. Bird was in an agitated mood and, according to his host, seemed 'distracted' and was 'pacing up and down' with a 'doomed look'. Jacques tried to reassure him, and gently advised him to 'get his head together because he wasn't thinking straight.' Derrick's friend would later say: 'At the end of the film I said I would call him tomorrow. The last thing he said to me was, "Do you think I'm paranoid?" I said, "You are, you're not going to jail for something like that". He just seemed to be in another world. He didn't seem himself. He seemed sad, I suppose. That last time I saw him he was like a zombie. He had been like that for a couple of days. Very quiet and definitely not normal.'

Bird left the Jacques house at 12.30 in the morning. At the doorway, as Jacques saw him off, the worried man mentioned the fact that he had a meeting with his solicitor later that day. Jacques wished him luck with it but Bird simply mumbled something under his breath and walked away.

The meeting Bird was referring to was with solicitor Kevin Commons. It was scheduled for 3pm on 2 June and his brother David was also due to attend but, of course, it would never take place. Friends of David Bird claim that both he and Commons had wanted to try and help Bird find a solution to his financial problems, a theory that seems to be supported by a statement issued by David's daughters after his death, stating that their father's 'only downfall was to try and help his brother'.

Marcus Nickson, Kevin Commons's business partner of 18 years, knew of the meeting and said that the solicitor, who had known the family for many years, had only been 'trying to help'. 'There was a meeting that afternoon,' he explained. 'David and [Commons] had been friends for many years and I think Derrick got into some difficulty. The likelihood was he was giving his services for free in helping someone who needed his help – Derrick I would imagine. He would only agree to help Derrick if he was absolutely certain there was no conflict between the families.'

Bob Cullen's versions of events would seem to affirm this. Cullen says that Bird had turned to his brother for help towards the end of 2009, and that David had arranged for him to see Commons. 'This must have been after Christmas,' he said. During this meeting Commons would tape Bird's words. Although this was done with both his knowledge and consent, and was standard practice for Commons, who always liked to make sure he had everything in order, Bird would later take issue with the recording of their interview. According to Cullen this action would sow a 'seed of paranoia in Derrick's mind'. 'He started to talk about how they were out to get his money off him,' Cullen asserted, 'how they wanted to stitch him up. He said he was going to jail. He kept talking about going to jail for four or fifteen years.'

A further meeting was arranged for Bird by David and Commons, this time with an accountant. Once again Bird's statements were taped, and once again he was unhappy with this. As Gary Kennett, another friend who had seen Bird on the eve of the killings, would later tell the press, Bird was now was deeply suspicious of the motivations of both his brother and of Commons. 'He couldn't get it out of his mind,' Kennett stated. 'He thought they were getting him to say things.' It was an accusation that friends of the pair would strenuously deny, saying that both men simply wanted to help the troubled man.

Commons and David may have had Bird's best interests at heart but the latter certainly didn't see it that way. According to Kennett, Bird became increasingly 'paranoid' and 'depressed' believing that David and Commons were now conspiring against him. 'He was convinced that if he turned up at this meeting they were going to put him down forever and take his money,' Kennett said. 'He was talking about taking his money out of his bank account and running away forever.' Some say that Bird was convinced that it had been David and Commons who were in cahoots, and that they had been the ones who had 'shopped' him to the Inland Revenue in the first place.

One other friend, from the scuba diving club, said that Bird was furious with the solicitor for not agreeing to lie to them on his behalf. Whether this is true or not has yet to be ascertained but what is clear, from the correspondence from K J Commons legal firm, discovered on Bird's kitchen table when the police raided his home after the shootings, is that there were official dealings between the men.

Another theory has it that the meeting had been set up in order to talk through the contents of Mary Bird's will. It is said that Bird had told friends some months ago that he hoped to be able to resolve the tax issue and pay off his debt with money due to him on his mother's death. It is alleged, however, that in past weeks – much to his alarm and subsequent chagrin – he had discovered that the lion's share of her estate, money that would be accrued on the sale of the family home in Ennerdale, had been left to his brothers.

Friends say this had caused a dispute between the twins. Bird was riled. David was irked by his bother's continued accusations that somehow he was trying to conspire against him. 'David was cheesed off with the whole thing,' a friend of his would attest. 'He said "money makes problems". But Derrick was much more exasperated by it. He thought David and his friends were talking behind his back about the will and he was getting done over.' It was later revealed in an article in the *Daily Express* newspaper that Bird had also been relying on a share in a late cousin's will, which he had hoped would relieve some of his debts. When the inheritance, said to be worth £27,000, failed to materialise, Bird apparently 'went off the rails'.

We will never really know what the real purpose of the meeting of 2 June was, for tragically the three men due to attend it that day would not live to tell the tale. But what is clear from the testimonials from the friends and colleagues Bird confided in is that he was dreading it. They say that he felt as though he was being pushed into a corner by David and Commons. One friend claimed that Bird believed that his twin would rather see him serve time than part with the money that he believed was rightfully his. Bird, who, at the best of times, didn't like it when people talked behind his back, was now intensely paranoid. In his mind far from trying to help him, David Bird and Kevin Commons were intent on causing his downfall. Was this the reason why he selected them as his first victims?

The fact that Bird carried out his murderous rampage on the day of the meeting has to hold some significance, but one has to wonder when Bird decided to seek retribution on the two men. Did he wake that morning and decide that he'd had enough? Or had he, as it's been suggested by some, been planning it for months? Was there any significance in him going to see his son and grandson that day – as if to make his final farewells? Was he passing on scuba equipment simply because he knew by then that he'd not need it again? For when he visited Garry Kennett at his allotment on the afternoon of 1 June and gave him his diving gear he is alleged to have said to him: 'You'll get more use from them than I will.'

Those questions remained unanswered but what can be ascertained is that by the time dusk settled that evening Derrick Bird appeared, in his own mind at least, to be a man who had run out of options. He would tell Kennett that he was running off to Thailand, to Cooper that he was 'going down', and as he left the rank that evening he shook hands with two of the drivers, simply saying, 'Goodbye, I'm going down.' The last person he spoke to as he left Whitehaven was friend and colleague Peter Leder. 'You won't see me again,' he'd said before making his way back to Rowrah in his car. 'I couldn't understand why had had said that,' Leder remarked. 'I realise now why he wouldn't see us again because of what's happened.'

CHAPTER SEVEN

Although it seems almost impossible to believe now, given the cold-blooded way in which Derrick Bird killed his twin brother, according to their family there had never been any real dispute between the two men. As stated previously, in a statement which was released through the police after David's body had been formally identified, his three daughters Rachel, 28, Tracey, 26 and 19-year-old Katie said that their father's 'only downfall' was to 'try and help his brother'. Paying tribute to a man they described as 'the nicest man you could ever meet' they said: 'We would like to say there was absolutely no family feud.'

Joy Ryan, a family cousin, who is close to Mary Bird, backed this up, claiming that their mother had never even seen the twins argue. 'They were often at their mother's house and always seemed to get on well,' Joy said. 'Mary never talked about them having problems, or of jealousy between them. She would have mentioned something like that if it was worrying her.' Joy Ryan conceded that there 'could have been a row' between the brothers on the previous night, but there certainly 'wasn't a feud'.

Another family member, Brian Spencer, also denied that there were problems between Derrick and David, saying that on the Saturday before the killings the two men had been together at a motoring event. According to Spencer the brothers had been up at the local scramble track testing out an off-road vehicle that David had just finished working on, and by all accounts they had a great time together 'driving around, laughing their heads off'. Spencer described the relationship between the brothers as 'warm', with no underlying problems.

Further to this, according to Rev Marshall, there had been a 'good lot of banter' when all three sons visited their mother for tea that Sunday. 'If the family realised there was a problem with Derrick they would have immediately leapt to help him. That's the sort of family they are,' he said. 'And if there was an underlying problem between them there seems to be nobody who can tell you what it was.'

Maybe the family is right. Maybe there was no long-running feud between the two men. Maybe they genuinely did have a good relationship and did get along, maybe there was even a bond between the brothers. But there can be no denying that in the run-up to the events of 2 June 2010, there was some grievance, even if this was simply in Derrick Bird's head, which would lead him to seek out his brother in the early hours of the morning of that momentous day and kill him in cold blood as he lay sleeping.

Though David and Derrick Bird were twins, there was nothing to suggest this on first meeting them. In terms of their appearance, their prospects, and their personalities they couldn't have been more different. While one was tall and lean, the other was short and stocky. David was prosperous, Derrick, as we know now, was not. The former mechanic was well known and liked for being gregarious and for his laidback attitude. Derrick, by contrast, was taciturn, and suffered from insecurities.

By all accounts the twins had been close in early life. As young boys they were often seen out playing together in the streets of Ennerdale or in the surrounding countryside, going off lamping with their father Joe. From an early age they shared a mutual interest in vehicles, whether it was Motocross or go-carting or simply playing around with engines: both were said to be 'petrol heads'. Though they were not identical as young boys, they both had thatches of blonde hair and cheeky smiles, so there was a strong resemblance, though this would fade as they got older.

According to former teacher Nan Wilson, who taught the boys at Ehenside, they had a good relationship and their parents were keen not to separate them when the time came for them to move from their local primary to secondary school. 'They stayed in the same class but had different sets of friends,' she told the *Mail on Sunday*. 'They were these two fair-haired lads. One tall, one smaller. You would never have looked at them and thought they were twins but they were very much a united team. They were typical farming land lads. They didn't have an interest in putting pen to paper.'

Nan Wilson, now 75, was also a neighbour of Bird's in Rowrah, and said their work could often be 'scrappy' and like many boys their age they liked to get up to mischief, though she insists that neither boy was 'vicious'. They simply weren't interested in what was going on in the classroom, she explained, and were happiest when they were outdoors. 'They'd rather be out lamping or on their bikes.'

The brothers – who both went under the nickname 'Birdy' – were typical 'Jack the Lads', she said. Happy boys who had enjoyed a normal and healthy childhood and even though they had their own traits – for example David was the more outgoing of the two, whilst Derrick was the more introverted – they were a team.

'When they were lads they were not so very different after all. They came from a good, loving home. They had a bond that twins had. And you think how could you lose that?' Ms Wilson said, reflecting on Derrick's murder of his brother, which had left her in tears.

When it was clear at the age of 16 that neither twin had any interest in furthering their education, they left Ehenside and it would be at this point that their lives began to diverge. 'It was almost as if, as they started to mature, they found they had less in common,' a contemporary of the brothers recalls.

'They didn't have an issue with one another, it's just they were becoming more their own people. They moved in different circles, they had different jobs – their lives simply seemed to be going in different directions. But no one thought that was odd. It's quite normal for that to happen to twins as they grow up.'

Much to their parents' pride and relief both boys found employment relatively easily and quickly. As Derrick started work as a joiner David, still passionate about cars, would take on an apprenticeship as a mechanic, joining a local car dealership called J Edgar and Sons, in Frizington. He had always been skilled in this area, showing promise as a boy even when he was tinkering around with odd bits of machinery that came his way, and so it seems that even at this young age he had already found his metier in life. In those first few months at the dealership he did well and became a popular and dependable member of the team.

From an early age David seemed to have his life mapped out. He had a fulfilling career, which he saw more as a vocation than a job, and it was one that he was not only good at but that he enjoyed. And then in 1980 he would go on to marry Susan, whom he had met when he was just 17 years old, and within two years they would have their first child, Rachel, to be followed by Tracey and then Katie.

David Bird was a committed family man. 'A loving husband, doting dad and granddad,' is how his daughters chose to remember him in the tribute they paid to him following his death, and friends have attested that he was a wonderful father. In the eulogy he gave at David Bird's funeral, Rev Marshall would speak of Susan's despair when, having bathed and changed her girls for bed at night, 'powdered and dressed in their baby grows' her husband would rush in from his workshop to kiss them goodnight without washing his hands, 'leaving great greasy hand-marks' all over their chests. She never had the heart to reprimand him; she was just thrilled that he was such a loving father. It is interesting to note that his daughters would describe him in their statement as a 'loving husband', for earlier this year he and Susan had actually separated. But the parting was said to be extremely amicable and the couple remained exceptionally close.

David had always been determined to provide well for his family and he didn't let them down. Skilled as a mechanic, sunny in disposition, David was popular within the trade, and with his customers too. One neighbour described him as 'really well-known' within the surrounding area. 'If you ever wanted help or you broke down or whatever David was the man you would call out,' they said. Given all these talents, few were surprised when David decided to start his own business, opening a garage at Fell Dyke.

His success within the trade and some shrewd investments along the way allowed David to move up the property ladder and the family lived in a certain amount of style. High Trees, the detached farmhouse on the outskirts of Lamplugh, where he died, was not only attractive to look at but was substantial in size. Set in four acres of land, where he liked to walk his beloved Labrador Jed, some neighbours have described the property as 'luxurious'. 'It was a lovely house,' one said. 'It had a very nice feel to it, but that was very much down to David as well. He was a very nice host. Very laidback. He'd be there, pipe in hand, always making jokes, playing with his dog.'

David purchased High Trees in 2002 but he would go on to make other successful property and land investments along the way, including an executive development of four detached houses on a piece of neighbouring land. Sold to a local developer in 2004, he netted a large profit on the sale price of £335,000 for each property.

The village of Lamplugh may only be a stone's throw from Rowrah but it is a world apart. Set on a hill, Lamplugh is a leafy and attractive village, whose residents are for the most part affluent. Rowrah sits in the valley below and, with its uniform terraces of pebble-dashed two-up, two-downs, lacks the character and desirability of its neighbour. Derrick Bird's own home was in stark contrast to that of his twin. With its shabby exterior, cracked paintwork and peeling wallpaper, the house was in need of modernisation. Bird's kitchen hadn't been updated for many years and, unlike High Trees, there was no four-acre garden for Bird to sit in should he fancy it. If the cab driver wanted to catch some sunshine on a hot day he would have to perch on his doorstep while the traffic swept by.

The brothers' circumstances were in marked contrast, but then Derrick Bird had been neither as fortuitous nor as prosperous as his twin. It hadn't always been that way however. When Derrick first started out as a joiner he did well enough for himself. He was skilled at his trade and, following his stint at the undertakers in Whitehaven, he went on to gain a full-time position at Sellafield.

As the main employer in the area a job at the nuclear plant had its benefits. It offered job security for starters and also the opportunity for promotion. A job there was very much seen to be a job for life, (many of Bird's victims, who had worked at the plant, had done so for the majority of their adult lives) and so when he was taken on by the plant his family had been extremely happy for him.

Like his twin, Derrick also found love early on, setting up home in his early twenties with his childhood sweetheart Linda Mills. He was said to be delighted when she fell pregnant for the first time. The arrival of Graeme in 1985 was a source of great celebration for Bird, for he now had a son to whom he could pass on his love of the outdoors, just as his own father had done when he was growing up, and he could also share his love of cars.

For a time things seemed to be going well for Bird, but it was not to last. He was dismissed from Sellafield in 1990 for theft of materials reported to be worth over £15,000. As a source would tell the newspapers: 'It was not just a screwdriver or a few screws. It was machinery. He was taking all sorts of equipment.' What prompted Bird to steal materials from his employers is unclear, but his subsequent conviction rattled him.

The fact that his father, Joe, was said to have been deeply shamed by the incident didn't help matters and would be a bone of contention between the pair. Joe had always prided himself in being an upstanding member of society and lived within the law. As far as he was concerned his younger son had not only disgraced himself but had called into question the good name of the family. Friends claim that over the years his son became increasingly bitter about the affair and felt that he had been treated unfairly by his former employers.

Even though the sentence was suspended Bird realised that he would find it hard to gain work as a joiner again. He had blotted his copybook and, without references to call on, had little choice other than to take on self-employed work. So he joined the cab rank at Whitehaven. He worked hard for his living but no longer had the prospects or the security that he'd enjoyed whilst working at Sellafield. As if life as a jobbing cabbie wasn't difficult enough for Bird to come to terms with, he suffered the further indignity of having to drive his former friends and colleagues around the area.

The disparity in the fortunes of David and Derrick Bird was stark and it would be understandable if Bird felt a degree of sibling rivalry even though he had been the cause of his own downfall. It can't have been easy to see his brother's life go from strength to strength as his simply drifted along. If Bird was embittered by that fact to start with then he was to be further galled when his father, in what he can only have perceived as a gesture of favouritism, lent David the sum of £25,000 towards the end of the nineties. It is believed that David needed the money to invest in his car repair business. The loan came to light when Joe Bird's will was uncovered at the Probate Registry, in London, days after the shootings.

The document shows that in 1997 Joe made a gift of £25,000 to his son on the condition that the same sum of money should be deducted from his share of the estate when it was divided up. The codicil – supplement to the will – stated: 'Having transferred money to my son David Bird, absolutely, I direct my son, the said David Bird, shall bring into hopscotch upon the division of my residuary estate the sum of £25,000.'

In principle there seems nothing wrong with this. Joe had helped out his son when he needed it, and in time and on his death Brian and Derrick would get their rightful share of their father's estate. But in practice it was not so straightforward, for when Joe died in 1998 his net estate was just £10,000. Debts and taxes had reduced his worth considerably. As his widow Mary would, along with the house in Ennerdale – which was hers for her lifetime – receive the money, Brian and Derrick were left with nothing. There is no record that David Bird ever paid the money back.

In the light of this it is easy to understand perhaps why Bird was so enraged to learn that he had apparently been sidelined in his mother's will when he learnt of its contents. For he had always believed that when she died, and the property in Ennerdale had been sold, that the situation would have been rectified. It appears that this was not to be the case.

It is unclear how the third brother, Brian, felt about the loan but friends say that it was a source of contention between the twins. Bird saw the loan as a deliberate act of favouritism towards his brother. Since his dismissal from Sellafield Derrick had struggled financially and even though his twin brother had experienced a few ups and downs with his business, he had generally prospered and lived comfortably. It was as though Joe saw David as the prodigal son.

There may have been no actual 'feud' between the men, but there were simmering tensions – on Derrick's part at least. And whilst they may have put on a united front at family gatherings, social events and in front of their mother Mary, it's clear that they weren't close. Even though they lived within just miles of each other Derrick and David didn't often meet and seemed to exist in different orbits. No one expected them to live in each other's pockets simply because they were twins, but according to friends they barely acknowledged one another's existence outside the family circle.

Ian Hewer, who holidayed with Bird in Thailand, said that as far as he knew Derrick had: 'Just one brother – his older brother Brian.' Whilst Michael Pugh, a driver friend of Bird's who had known him for 15 years, was completely oblivious to the fact that the future killer had a brother at all, let alone a twin. And it seems the reticence to acknowledge one another went both ways. Marcus Nickson, Kevin Commons's business partner and as such a long standing friend of David's, would attest that: 'I hardly knew of Derrick because David rarely even mentioned him.'

David and Derrick Bird, may on the face of it have been 'chalk and cheese' in terms of their physical appearance, their prospects and their finances. They may not have moved in the same circles or felt much obligation to see each other outside their family circle but they had things in common which should have run deeper. They were family men: sons, fathers and grandfathers. They shared the same passions – cars, Motocross and a love of the great outdoors. They were community-spirited and neighbourly. But, above all, they were brothers.

CHAPTER EIGHT

'Kind', 'ordinary', 'sociable', 'nice' and 'an ordinary guy' are just some of the words Derrick Bird's fellow cab drivers at the taxi rank in Whitehaven would use to describe their colleague following the events of 2 June. Having worked as a driver, touting for work at this rank for over 20 years, Bird was not only a well-known member of the crew but he was also well liked.

When he wasn't running a fare, and when it wasn't raining, he would be seen out in Duke Street leaning against his parked car enjoying a quick coffee, joshing around with fellow drivers or engaged in banter with locals from the town as he waited to collect his next fare. He was a familiar face, a 'friendly fellow', a 'good driver' and a 'good guy to work with'. He had friends on the rank. Some were simple acquaintances – people he would exchange pleasantries with, others were drinking pals who'd happily join him for a pint at the end of a shift. And then there were his close friends – the ones he holidayed with, or confided in about his financial worries, such as Mark Cooper, who Bird had talked with on the evening of 1 June.

But the rank was where he opened fire on those same friends, turning Duke Street and its surrounding roads into a murder scene. Paul Williams, Don Reid and Terry Kennedy were all targets of his, as was Darren Rewcastle, who would die in the carnage. Those friends who witnessed the proceedings and watched a much-loved member of their crew die in front of them would be traumatised. Those who heard of the shootings were left baffled and bemused as to why their colleague would turn on them in such a violent way.

Even in the aftermath of the shootings few were able to terms with notion that the man they knew simply as 'Birdy' was now one of Britain's most notorious mass murderers. He had been their colleague, their peer, a friend, their drinking partner, a travelling companion. Now he was simply a killer.

'I used to go for a pint with him on Sunday night,' James Healde, 48, said. 'He was quiet but sociable, like. Always good company, always asking about you.'

He was popular with his regular customers too. One woman who had used his cab for 12 years told the *Whitehaven News and Star* newspaper that 'he was a kind and thoughtful person. He was always friendly and always had a smile on his face and would go out of his way to make everybody around him happy'. Even Paul Wilson, whom Bird shot in the cheek when he pulled up alongside him outside the police station on Scotch Street, found it hard to reconcile the notion that the man he had known and liked for some time and the person who pulled the trigger of a gun at him were one and the same person. He would tell the press that Bird 'is still my friend' – referring to him in present tense.

If the drivers stationed at the Duke Street rank generally along well, there had been a growing amount of tension between the drivers over recent months which had culminated in a series of disputes and bust-ups between them. Whitehaven is not a large town and with over 150 cab drivers working there, there was hardly enough business to go round, especially in the quieter months when the tourists weren't there. The recession had taken its toll on the business and this, coupled with the regulation of taxis in 2008, had meant that the drivers were taking home half of what they were used to.

For a man who was already suffering from serious financial problems this was, of course, not an ideal situation for Bird to find himself in. And, as if that wasn't enough, rising unemployment in and around Whitehaven had meant that there was a flood of new drivers now working on the rank.

'There are just too many drivers and not enough fares to go round,' a Whitehaven cabbie explained. 'Birdy had been working here for years and he believed these guys were taking business from him.' According to another source the local drivers were also riled about the fact that cabbies were coming in from outside of the area, from Blackpool and Preston, to tout for work in Whitehaven. Competition at the rank had become fierce and, as a result, tensions were running high. In the weeks leading up to the killings there had been a number of arguments at the rank, which Bird had been involved in.

In the past there had been a gentleman's agreement between the drivers in Duke Street. Each cab would wait in line for the fare, gradually moving up the queue until it was their turn to collect a punter. A new cab driving entering town would have to join the back of the queue and wait their turn. It is a system used by cab drivers in towns and cities all over the country and, for as far back as anyone in Duke Street can remember, it was one that they practised, but in recent weeks some of the drivers had started to renege on the pact.

Desperate times called for desperate measures, and, with the out-of-town drivers operating this way, some of the regulars decided to do the same. According to Mark Cooper it had been going on for months and complaints had been made about the practice to the local council. He claimed that everyone was at it. It wasn't fair, it wasn't right, but some felt they had little choice. 'It was a case of if you can't beat 'em you might as well join 'em,' another driver explained.

'There was a lot of bad feeling down on the rank,' driver Michael Pugh explained.

But Bird, who had worked at this rank for over 20 years, didn't see it that way. He was enraged by what was going on. To find that drivers were 'stealing' business from him, was effectively like discovering they were stealing money from him. Colleagues said he was growing increasingly frustrated with the situation and, as one of the longest serving cabbies on the rank, believed that he should put an end to it. He exchanged words with some of the 'queue jumpers'.

Steven Pater, 27, had seen Bird on the Saturday before the shootings. 'Birdy was always complaining about drivers touting for business instead of going to the rank and waiting,' he explained. 'When I last saw him in Whitehaven he was really drunk, which was unusual because he'd normally be out driving at that time. I called over to say I'd drive him home and he replied, "No I'm going to sort this out". I'm not surprised he's lost it over this because it's been going on for months and he's been under a lot of financial pressure as a result.'

Bird did nothing that night but on Tuesday 1 June he got involved in an argument with a handful of the drivers. Having spoken to Mark Cooper about his tax problem Bird is then said to have had words with a couple of the drivers. The row was 'heated' with voices raised. Witnesses say it was not resolved, and when Bird stormed off that evening his parting line to the group was: 'There's going to be a rampage tomorrow!' As Bird walked down the rank back to his car he shook hands with some of the other drivers saying,

'Goodbye, you'll not see me again.' He then got into the car and drove slowly past the rank, staring menacingly at the drivers he had argued with. 'Someone said something to him and he took it to heart,' said a driver, who wanted to remain anonymous.

As strange as Bird's behaviour was, no one took what he said to heart. They simply thought it was something said in the heat of the moment. No one thought he was serious. Yet while Bird was usually mild-mannered and placid he was known to fly off the handle at times too, especially when pushed. But everyone assumed that Bird would go home, calm down and be back to his normal self the following day.

But Bird, of course, didn't do that. And when he returned to town the following morning to seek revenge on those he believed had wronged him he also took pot shots at drivers he got on with, such as Paul Williams and Don Reed. However it was Darren Rewcastle who Bird seemed intent on killing.

Some of the drivers at the rank were perplexed as to why Bird wanted to 'single' Rewcastle out. The two men were friends, they said. They had holidayed together and, according to other drivers, used to enjoy a 'josh' and joke together. Glenda Pears, manager of L&G Cabs on Duke Street, confirmed that the two were friends. 'They used to stand and have a craic on the rank. [Rewcastle] was friends with everybody and used to stand and joke on the street.'

'Darren was Darren,' Paul Williams said. 'Everyone got on with him.' Everyone other than Derrick Bird it seemed. It is not known whether Rewcastle had been involved in the flare-up at the rank on 1 June, but other drivers said that he and Bird had argued about the issue before. Rewcastle certainly wasn't the only driver who had occasionally jumped the queue but, according to his colleagues, he was the type of person who would have stood up to Bird in an argument and wouldn't have put up 'with his nonsense'. Rewcastle was known to be a 'bit of a joker', a 'number one wind-up merchant' and a 'man who told it as it was'. If words were exchanged between the two men could it be the case that Rewcastle, whether intentionally or not, had said something to Bird which pushed him over the edge?

But some friends say that there was another motive behind the killing of Rewcastle: this was that Bird had believed that he was having an affair with ex-partner Linda Mills, an accusation that was completely untrue and 'all in Bird's head'. Was it this unfounded suspicion that riled Bird so much that his former friend and colleague would become his third victim?

Driving a cab may have not been Derrick Bird's first choice of career but it was a job that he was good at and enjoyed. The money may not have been great, it may not have offered either job security or prospects but it had certain benefits. For starters it meant that Bird was his own boss and was thus in charge of his time, which would allow him to pursue his other interests: diving and Motocross and taking long-haul trips abroad. Not only did he like being behind the wheel of a car but it had given him a social life and he enjoyed talking to customers. But in 2007 an event occurred that was not only to alter his view of the job but, according to friends, was to change him forever.

Bird had driven a group of teenagers to Moor Row but when he stopped the car, rather than paying the fare they jumped out of the vehicle and ran off. Bird gave chase but when he caught up with one of them, Daniel Carr, and challenged him, the teenager hit him in the face. Bird fell to the ground and was knocked unconscious, losing two teeth in the process.

When the case came to court in 2007, Bird explained to magistrates how the incident had left him 'nervous and anxious' and that he had become 'terrified' of working late at night. Carr admitted causing actual bodily harm and was ordered to pay £250 compensation to Bird, as well as £175 in costs.

In the weeks that followed the attack Bird was so shaken by the incident he had started to drink heavily, as though he was trying to blot out the memory of what had happened.

John McDonald, a fellow cab driver, said in an interview he gave to Channel 4 that the events of that night had a significant impact on Bird. Not only had he 'smashed his skull' when he fell to the pavement, leaving him with a gash at the back of the head, but McDonald also confirmed that after the attack Bird had started to drink more. When he saw the future killer in Whitehaven on the weekend before the shootings, Bird was so drunk he was 'bouncing off the walls'. 'That wasn't Derrick,' McDonald said simply.

Some friends have said that Bird never really recovered from the assault and that it had scarred him emotionally. 'He was never really the same after that. It changed him forever,' they said.

CHAPTER NINE

With his circle of friends, the relationships he had with his sons and his many interests Derrick Bird was by no means a loner; but he was lonely. Photographs of Bird's kitchen, taken by the police after the shootings, are telling. On the kitchen table sits a solitary un-cleared plate from which he must have eaten one of his final meals. In front of that stands an array of condiments next to a pile of official correspondence – including a letter from Kevin Commons's legal firm. Two of the metal-framed kitchen chairs around the table are stacked on top of one another and in general the place looks as though it is need of a thorough clean.

This is not a room where you can imagine the 52-year-old entertaining family and friends, or even a girlfriend. It seems to serve a single purpose –as a place for Derrick Bird to eat, drink coffee and brood over his numerous woes. The backdrop to the life of a solitary man, who was said to be plagued by bouts of loneliness.

It was not always this way, of course, for there had been a time in Derrick Bird's life when he had known both love and happiness, and that was when he first set up home with his childhood sweetheart Linda Mills, the mother of his two sons, Graeme and Jamie.

The couple had met when they attended Ehenside Secondary School where Bird was two years Linda's senior. It has never been ascertained as to whether they were married or not. A certificate has never been found. But whatever their official status was, for a time Derrick and Linda were very much a couple.

Friends of Linda, whom they describe as a 'lovely woman' and a 'wonderful woman' have since questioned how much the couple had in common. With Derrick not 'being one for much conversation', Linda was said to be the more outgoing and sociable of the pair, but for a time at least they seemed happy enough with one another and were both said to be delighted when Linda fell pregnant with their first child, Graeme, in 1985. However, as time went on their relationship is known to have become strained and in 1994, a few months after the birth of their second son Jamie, they separated.

Sadly the separation was a stressful one. Linda took custody of the boys but on the days that Bird had access to his children he would sit in his car, beeping his horn to signal his arrival rather than face his ex at the front door. Some have said that Bird still pined for Linda, who became a housekeeper at a holiday resort in Penrith, and that after the separation he would sometimes drive to her village at night and sit outside her house in his car. Again, this could just be hearsay but what can be said is that her departure caused a void in Bird's life, one that he would spend the next 16 years trying to fill.

Friends say that Bird liked the company of women but that sadly he didn't have much success with them. Short in stature, tubby, and with thinning hair, he didn't exactly stand out in a crowd and as a result he never felt completely relaxed in women's company. Rather than try and engage the females he met in the pubs and bars around West Cumbria in conversation he would simply ogle them and, as such, gained a reputation of being something of a 'letch' when it came to the opposite sex. Pub landlord and diving companion Bob Cullen said of his friend: 'He used to just stare at them. We used to take the [piss], but it wasn't pleasant. His nickname among the lads was "the dog".'

Bird's diving friends weren't the only ones who would mock the 52-year-old for his lack of luck with women. Down at the cab rank in Whitehaven it had become something of a long-standing joke amongst the drivers who would tease 'Birdy' about the fact that he was single. 'They used to wind him up because he was a really quiet lad and kept himself to himself,' a driver said. 'They would tease him about lasses and say they have had better runs than him.' The driver insisted that it was just 'friendly banter' but Bird was sensitive about the subject and he would at times take it to heart.

Over the years there had been a couple of women in Derrick's life but none of these relationships were lasting. One such woman was Judith Fee, a 52-year-old care worker, who had dated Bird for a while at beginning of the decade. Judith ended the relationship when her sister died from cancer. She had hoped that he might provide a shoulder to cry on, be there to support her, but when she broke the news to him he apparently told her, 'That's life'.

Fee went on to see John McStraw, a friend from the Solway Sub-Aqua Club, whom Bird had introduced Fee to six years before in a local pub. When word got back to the cab driver that Fee and McStraw were an item he was said to have been distressed.

The mother of three would tell the *Sun*: 'He seemed jealous and started ringing me. He told me he was depressed about me and Johnny being together. He said he would take me back. He promised me everything.' Fee also claimed to be disturbed when she and McStraw later bumped into Bird when they were holidaying in Lanzarote, saying that she felt like he was stalking her. 'Him and his mates from the Solway Sub-Aqua Club were planning a trip to Egypt but he changed their mind to go to Lanzarote – where we were,' she told the newspaper.

When the couple subsequently became engaged Judith decided not to tell Bird, for fear of how he would take the news and so when she first heard the news of the killing spree she feared for her life. 'Johnny's best man was out with Derrick the week before. I was really frightened, thinking, "Did he tell Derrick about the wedding?" I was so scared I couldn't even hold the phone. I didn't leave her house till I knew it was over. It could have been me or one of my children,' she said to the *Sun*.

Unable to find love or a stable relationship back home Bird cast his eye further afield – to the exotic shores of Thailand to be precise. As we know Derrick was a passionate diver and each year he would try and get away with fellow members of the Solway dive club on a trip abroad. As much as he loved diving round the Lake District, nothing could beat the lure of diving in the sea itself, and so this would be the highlight of the year for Bird. In recent years he and his friends had taken trips to Croatia, Egypt, the Canary Islands and Thailand.

With its clear blue waters, its reefs, climate and white sandy beaches it was easy to see why Bird, as a diving fanatic, would fall in love with Thailand. It was also a world away from the greyness of his life in Rowrah and his problems. But there was something else that would attract Bird to the country and that was its women. Not only were they as beautiful and exotic as the island itself, but they were available, even to a man like Bird. In the haunts and clubs that Bird and his friends used to frequent in Pattaya, south east of Bangkok, so long as you had enough money in your wallet you could command the attention of many a pretty girl.

By day Bird and his crew, who called themselves the 'Bad

Boys', would go diving or would visit the Pattaya Shooting Club, where they spent hours on the shooting ranges, firing high calibre revolvers and pump-action shotguns. By night they would head out along the main strip, drinking in bars and meeting women.

Terry Kennedy, the driver who Bird shot during the rampage in Duke Street and who had accompanied him to Thailand on more than one occasion, said: 'He chatted to girls in the bars,' Kennedy said. 'He bought them drinks, took a couple back to the hotel – nothing outrageous or out of the ordinary.'

Bird began to get a taste for the local girls. According to Chris Bulmer, former owner of one of their favourite bars on Pattaya Beach, Spicy Girls A-Go-Go, Bird had first come to the island in 2003. 'He used to go to Thailand for the women,' said one source. By 2007 'women' had become 'woman'. She reportedly went by the name of 'Hon' – although this is suspected to be a pseudonym – and by all accounts was extremely pretty. 'Hon looked about 19 but I think she was about 30 at the time,' Terry Kennedy, who had been on the particular trip, explained. 'I knew Derrick liked the lass so I told him to go for it, he had nothing to lose.' But Kennedy may have underestimated the extent of Bird's feelings towards Hon for, as it would later transpire, his infatuation with her would cost him a great deal.

According to Chris Bulmer, Bird spent his days diving on that five-week trip and at night would try and woo Hon with presents and drinks. 'He became obsessed,' Bulmer went on. 'He loved her and whenever he came back he would immediately compensate the bar and take her away. She was his and that's how he saw it.'

Bulmer says that if Hon wasn't at Spicy Girls when Bird asked to see her he would fly off in a rage. 'He would get very angry if he couldn't see his girl,' the bar owner added. 'He could be so quiet and mild-mannered and then he could just flip.'

On his return to Cumbria that year Bird would try and continue his 'relationship' with Hon. Not only would be bombard the girl with texts, emails and letters but he sent her gifts and money too – 'hundreds of pounds of his savings', a friend said. Bird, it seemed, was obsessed.

Some reports suggest that during that trip Hon had become increasingly concerned about the degree of interest Bird was showing in her and that she had quit working at the club for a while in order to get some space.

'I heard he was sending her things,' Bulmer said. 'It was always something I warned my customers about. These are working girls and they are not interested in relationships.'

But Bird didn't see it like that. As far was he was concerned he *was* in a relationship with Hon and it was one that he wanted to pursue. In the many messages he sent her he would talk of returning to Thailand soon to see her. And only the previous year he had tried to make that trip but, following a drunken scuffle with a friend during their stopover in Qatar, before boarding a connecting flight to Bangkok, Bird was detained by security officers. They deemed him to be unfit to fly and in the end he was deported back to England.

Bird had spoken to his friends about the relationship. At the cab rank in Duke Street they mocked him about it, teasing him about his 'little Thai woman'. But Bird wasn't happy to be made fun of in this way. As far as he was concerned he and Hon had a genuine future and so when she told him that she would come to England and live with him he was over the moon. It was everything he ever wanted and now it actually seemed to be coming true.

Believing that they were not only in a relationship but had a future too, just weeks before the shootings Bird, despite all his financial worries, sent Hon £1000. 'It was a hell of a lot of money for a taxi driver,' a friend from the ranks said. 'And then he heard nothing from her for days.'

When Bird eventually did hear back from Hon it was not the message he had been waiting for. There was no appreciation of gift, no apology for not texting him sooner, not even a thank-you. Just a single line telling him never to contact her again and that she was seeing someone else. Hon never made any reference to the money and would subsequently make no attempt to return it.

'She had no interest in him whatsoever,' the friend said. 'He felt like such a mug. Derrick said he'd been made a fool out of, he couldn't believe it.'

But Derrick Bird felt more than just a 'mug'. He was devastated. It didn't help that the lads at the taxi rank would rib him mercilessly about it. Bird would allow them their jokes for a while but some say that it was all getting too much for him. In public he may have put a brave face on it but inside he had been torn apart. His dream – one of the only things that kept him going – had been shattered. Robbed of money, hope and his chance of happiness, he was a broken man and friends say he fell into a deep depression.

CHAPTER TEN

To those that knew him Derrick Bird was kind and affable, friendly and sociable, the kind of man who would happily stop and greet you in the street when you passed him by. But we know now that beyond the cheery smile, the sunny disposition, lay a man in turmoil.

One of the questions that would be asked time and time again in the weeks that followed the shootings was why hadn't anyone picked up on Derrick Bird's state of mind? Surely, with all his mounting problems and worries, someone close to him must have realised that this was a man who was close to breaking point?

Derrick Bird was not a loner; he didn't keep himself to himself. He had regular contact with his family, he socialised, he was on friendly terms with his work colleagues and neighbours. Someone within his circle must have seen that he was going through some kind of breakdown? Apparently not. And the reason for this is simple. Derrick Bird didn't want anyone to see beyond the smile. He didn't want people to know the extent of his troubles and his woes. He hid his problems away from the world, just as he had done with his money.

This is not to say that Bird didn't share his worries with his family and friends. He did. We know that he spoke to Mark Cooper, Bob Cullen and Neil Jacques about his tax issues. He chose to confide in Terry Kennedy and another driver from the rank about his problems with his Thai 'girlfriend' Hon and her subsequent treatment of him. Kevin Commons, the family lawyer, had been aware of his financial issues and the fact that he was being investigated by the Inland Revenue. His twin brother David would have known that Derrick had issues with his mother's will and the fact that he believed he had been cheated out of his inheritance. And this in itself is key, for Derrick Bird never painted the whole picture to any one person. He would compartmentalise his difficulties, sharing only one problem at a time, with one person at a time. No one ever heard the full story and he wanted to keep it that way.

When the family of Derrick Bird said that they hadn't the faintest clue as to what had driven him to commit his crimes, we have to believe them. For in the eyes of Mary, Brian, Graeme and Jamie Bird, Derrick didn't have any issues. As far as they were concerned he was just a devoted son, loving brother and father. He may not have had the luck and fortune in life of his twin but he seemed happy enough and that was the image he was keen to present to them. A sense of pride would have prevented Bird from sharing the full extent of his troubles with the people he loved most in the world. He wouldn't have wanted his sons to know that he was being investigated for tax evasion and possibly faced a prison sentence. He didn't tell Brian of his financial problems and he would never let on to Mary that he had issues with his twin. He kept these secrets well away from his family and they would only learn of them on his death.

Rev Marshall said that there had been a great deal of family 'banter' between the three brothers when they visited Mary for tea on the Sunday before the killings. One can only assume that this is an accurate picture. Derrick Bird wouldn't allow anyone round that table – with the exception of David – to know what was really going on his head, and even then his twin would only have known part of the story. Instead he would keep up the act, pretending there was nothing wrong. That afternoon he was the dutiful son, the loving brother. None of them would ever realise that he had reached boiling point.

It was only when Bird was drunk that the façade would come down. Only then would the dark secrets that plagued his mind come to light. *In vino veritas*, as they say, but even then he would only drip-feed his audience one problem at a time, never give them the whole picture.

But the problem of keeping issues like these to oneself is that after a time they start to fester and this is what appears to have happened in the case of Derrick Bird. Small aggravations would be blown out of all proportion. The tiniest slight became a gross injustice. A casual remark or a rebuke would be taken to heart and not forgotten. And out of all this, serious grudges would be born, scores that Derrick Bird would want to settle.

When Jason Carey, the diving instructor from the Solway Sub-Aqua Club, had reprimanded Bird for taking a novice diver into deep water, for example, he hadn't done so out of malice or because he had a personal issue with the 52-year-old. He had told him off simply because he had put the novice diver in a potentially hazardous situation. However, Bird hadn't seen it that way. But rather than being irritated or smarting from the episode, we are told by members of the diving club that Bird 'hated' Carey as a result.

Likewise when Darren Rewcastle stood up to Bird when he accused him of queue-jumping at the rank, rather than answering back or just letting it go, the troubled man brooded over it to such an extent that he would later kill him. As one driver noted: 'The whole issue of queue-jumping was really annoying but it [wasn't] something that would cause you to want to kill someone over.'

Some friends say that over the last few months of his life Bird was becoming increasingly paranoid. He couldn't bear it if he thought people were talking about him behind his back, or discussing his business in any way. Is this why he took against his brother and Kevin Commons, and would

Flowers left by the gate of the home of Derrick Bird's first victim:
his twin brother, David.

Above left: Derrick Bird, the 'quiet' 52-year-old taxi driver who killed 12 people and injured 11 others.

©*Rex Features*

Above right and *below*: Bird pictured on a diving holiday to Egypt in 2008.

©*Getty Images*

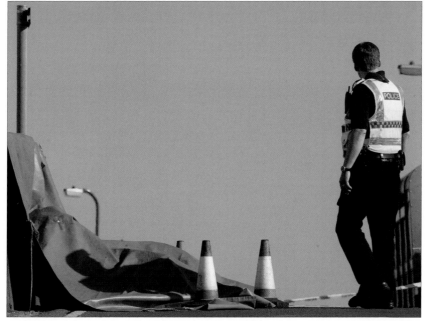

Above: Police cordon off Duke Street in Whitehaven on the day of the shootings.
©Getty Images

Below: An officer at the scene of one of Bird's three murders in Seascale.
©Getty Images

Bird left a trail of devastation.

Above left: An armed officer stands in a wooded area near the hamlet of Boot, where Derrick Bird finally ended his rampage by killing himself.

©Getty Images

Above right: Bird's home in Rowrah.

Below: Floral tributes at the taxi rank on Duke Street, Whitehaven, where Derrick Bird shot at former colleagues, killing one and injuring two others.

©Getty Images

The innocent victims (*left to right*): David Bird, Darren Rewcastle, Susan Hughes, Kenneth Fishburn, Garry Purdham, and a photograph of the home of Derrick Bird's solicitor, Kevin Commons, who he also murdered that day.

© *Getty Images*

Jennifer and James Jackson, Jamie Clark, Michael Pike, Isaac Dixon and flowers left at the scene of the murder of Jane Robinson, Bird's final victim.

©Getty Images

United in grief. Crowds gather to pay tribute to the victims at a service in Seascale on the first Sunday after the shootings (*above*). Prayers were said and tributes were laid at a temporary memorial (*below*).

choose to kill them on the morning of the meeting? Marcus Nickson, Commons' business partner and David Bird's three daughters Rachel, Tracey and Katie, attest that all David and Commons had wanted to do was to 'help' Bird. But once again he hadn't seen it that way. In his mind he believed that they were not only trying to 'stitch' him up and 'take all [his] money' but that they had been the ones who had shopped him to the Inland Revenue in the first place.

And then there is the situation regarding his mother. Neighbours say that Bird had become terribly depressed about her illness. She had been treated for cancer and no sooner had she recovered from that than she suffered a stroke. Derrick and his mother had always been close and friends say that in many respects he was a better son to her than David, in that he was more attentive. His daily visits meant the world to her and he would say to Rev Marshall that he believed that popping round for tea each day gave her a sense of purpose. But it could just as easily be argued that Bird derived as much pleasure from the visits as she did. By visiting his mother every day, by making himself almost indispensable to her, he was giving himself a sense of purpose too. Those visits must have brought comfort to him as well, for spending time in the company of Mary Bird must have filled a void in his life. Little wonder he was 'depressed' at the thought of losing her.

As his mood grew darker Bird also seemed to lose his sense of humour as well as his grip on reality. There had always been 'a great deal of banter' down on the rank at

Duke Street. There was a slightly macho atmosphere there at times and all the drivers came in for a fair share of ribbing, whether it was to do with their love lives, their appearance or winding each other up about the football. According to the drivers there it was never anything serious or vicious, just harmless japery to amuse them whilst they waited for fares. And for a time Bird had rather enjoyed the camaraderie that came with that. We know that he and Rewcastle liked to 'josh' together and he liked Darren's wisecracks.

However, lately Derrick had started to take it all to heart. He no longer liked it when they chuckled about his lack of prowess with women, when they took the mickey out of him for being tight with money, when they laughed about his Thai girlfriends or teased him for taking money off his elderly mother. And when they laughed when he told them about Hon and the money he had sent her he felt particularly ridiculed by their jokes.

Bird had always been a social drinker. He didn't drink every night, for he was often on a shift driving during evening hours, but two or three nights a week he could be found at one of his locals enjoying a pint or two in convivial company. But after the attack on Moor Row friends say his alcohol intake went up. Rather than sticking to two or three pints in an evening he would binge-drink.

Although these episodes were few and far between when they did occur they stuck in people's minds. There was the incident the year before, mentioned in the previous chapter, when Bird was detained by security officers at Qatar airport.

Bird had been flying out to Thailand for a holiday and to see Hon, but on the flight from England to Qatar, where they had a stopover, he is said by his travelling companion to have consumed a vast quantity of alcohol.

'I wasn't drinking but he was,' his co-traveller said. 'He kept ordering two drinks at a time. Then he'd fall asleep for a bit and wake up, ring the buzzer and ask for more.' By the time Bird reached Qatar he was said to be 'wasted', so much so that he hit a friend at the airport. Security officials deemed that Bird was unfit to fly and suggested that he waited at the airport until he sobered up. His friends travelled on without him, but in the interim Bird is said to have had a subsequent altercation with the security guards, and after being held overnight, he was deported back to the UK the following day. Devastated not to make it to Thailand where he could see Hon, humiliated by the turn of events, Bird was thought to be very depressed about the incident. Then last winter, following a drinking binge, Bird was said to be so drunk that he fell over in the snow and stayed there until the morning, when he eventually came round.

No one is suggesting for a moment that it was alcohol that would send Bird over the edge. According to the testimonial given by Neil Jacques, who Bird had seen on the evening prior to the shootings, the strongest thing that passed their lips all night was coffee. But what is of interest perhaps is why Bird's drinking patterns had changed. Could it be that Bird was no longer drinking for pleasure, but to forget?

Bob Cullen said that when Bird drank, another side to his personality emerged. 'When he was drunk he used to get moody and broody. There was a dark side to him,' he said. Back in September 2009 the two men had holidayed together and Cullen says: 'When we were in Croatia he told us, "one of these days I'm going to get a gun and shoot them all".' Cullen and his friends ignored Bird. They knew he was drunk and dismissed anything he said as gibberish. 'Of course we didn't believe him,' he said. 'We told him not to be so stupid.'

Whether Bird was already planning his deadly rampage as early as September 2009 is uncertain, but the incident throws light on the state of Bird's mind even back then.

Karen Lewis, a 47-year-old prostitute who claimed to have sex with Bird in October 2005, said that her client had revealed a dark side to his personality after their encounter. She claimed that Bird, whom she met in Coventry's Red Light District and had paid her £30 for the evening, told her how much he hated his family. 'He spoke of hating his brother, of being so much in debt he couldn't crawl out of it,' she recalled. 'He didn't like the people where he lived. He said when he shoots them he'd know which ones to do because there were people in the village that he absolutely couldn't stand.' Despite only meeting Bird once, Lewis said that his chilling words had stayed with her all this time and she had been unable to shake the encounter from her mind.

It has yet to be established whether Bird ever sought professional help to deal with his numerous problems. Some initial reports suggested that he had in his possession a prescription for antidepressants, whilst another alleged that he tried to get help from a medical centre on the night before the shootings, only to be turned away, though neither story has been corroborated.

According to the *Independent* newspaper there is the possibility that Bird had been self-harming for some time and that the telltale wounds had been discovered during a post-mortem on the cab driver. They allege that an 'insider at an advice body helping sufferers' had claimed that the police had been in contact with them 'in relation to Derrick Bird' saying that that they had 'found evidence of years of self-harm to his body'. One can only speculate as to whether, had Bird had received psychiatric help, the events of 2 June 2010 might have been averted.

Many of Derrick Bird's friends acknowledge the fact that he had a problem or two, saying that was the reason why he could be prone to being 'quiet', 'moody' or 'maudlin' at times. They say he was 'troubled' about being investigated by the Inland Revenue, 'terrified' at the prospect of going to jail, that he 'resented' his brother, was 'suspicious' of the intentions of Kevin Commons, 'depressed' about his mother's health, 'irritated' by what was going on at the cab rank, 'humiliated' by Hon's treatment of him, 'devastated' that the relationship was over.

If you were to take any one of these emotions in isolation, difficult as they might be to cope with, it wouldn't be enough to give you a reason to kill. But when you add them all together it is clear to see why Derrick Bird reached breaking point.

CHAPTER ELEVEN

There is a specific term used by criminologists to define a person who embarks on a murderous rampage, taking multiple lives within a small space of time. This is a 'spree killer'. According to the FBI, a spree killer is someone who commits two or more murders, at several locations, without having what they describe as a 'cooling off period'.

Furthermore, spree killings tend not to follow any discernable pattern.

Having assassinated twelve people between 5.30am and 11.30am, at several locations within a 43-mile radius, Derrick Bird fits into this category. Unlike, for instance, a 'serial killer', whose murders are carried out one by one, at different times and locations, or the 'mass murderer' who kills multiple people at once in a single assault in one location, such as by setting off a bomb, the spree killer embarks on a journey to kill, without hesitation. And unlike the serial killer who lures his victims to their death, the spree killer hunts them down. Some of the people he kills along the way will be known to him, some he will personally bear a grudge against, some will simply serve as symbols for a perceived injustice. Others he will simply kill at random, although even then each of these victims will represent someone who has turned against him. The spree killer knows that in making such a public statement he will get caught in the end and so will usually try and take his own life at the end of the rampage.

On 1 June 2010 Derrick Bird went to bed a cab driver, a father of two, a brother, a son, a colleague and a friend, an 'ordinary man' according to everyone. But when he woke in the early hours of the morning he had become something else entirely. He was a spree killer: a man intent on avenging certain people he had issues with, of bringing the world to rights through murder, and of killing at random, because during that one moment in time he thought that it was his God-given right.

The actions of Derrick Bird closely mimic the behavioural patterns of a typical spree killer, as defined by psychologists and criminologists alike. He specifically chose to carry out his rampage in and amongst his local community, using his locality as the scene of his crime. He earmarked certain people who he wanted to avenge: his brother, his lawyer, a colleague and a friend he felt had wronged him (although Jason Carey would survive). And then he took his anger, anguish and rage against the world out on others. The fact that he took aim at fellow taxi drivers who he was not at odds with is worth noting.

It wasn't who they were it was what they stood for. In his mind they symbolised the problems he was having at work. Though it has baffled some, his willingness to turn his gun on complete strangers, people he had never met, is not unusual. By then pumped up by adrenalin stimulated by the killings, and fuelled with further rage, these people to Bird would symbolise his hatred towards life itself.

It is perhaps interesting to note that Bird didn't take aim at Iris Carruthers when he met her on the road that morning, after having killed his brother. It was only when Bird felt that he had taken out the three main people that had wronged him: David Bird, Kevin Commons and Darren Rewcastle, that he was able to start taking aim at others – the cab drivers, Susan Hughes, Isaac Dixon and the Jacksons to name just a few.

And as is often the case in the behavioural pattern of a spree killer, Derrick Bird would then take his own life. One final act of control.

Spree killers are not uncommon. We often hear stories from around the world of people walking into their workplace and venting their rage on colleagues by killing them; of college students rampaging through campuses and indiscriminately killing friends and lecturers, and, more shockingly, of troubled school children murdering their classmates and teachers in their educational establishments simply as an act against the institution itself.

And with all these stories comes a sense of shock and disbelief that this could happen here, to them, within their community, and with that comes the testimonial that they simply don't understand what can have led their friend/colleague/classmate to behave that way, for they had always seemed so 'normal', 'happy', 'stable', 'ordinary' even – just like Derrick Bird. It is only after the event when we learn how the murderer was disgruntled at work, had missed out on promotion, had been fired, or was facing bankruptcy that we see the fuller picture.

When the teenager's diary is read, and we realise they felt that they were different, that they didn't fit in, were excluded. Or we learn from email correspondence or social networking pages that a college student's heart had been broken or that they constantly felt like an outsider or a nobody. Only then do we open our eyes and see their turmoil. Only then do we understand why the switch flicked.

And it would be fair to say that this is what we, and the people of Cumbria who had nothing but nice words to say about him, did with Derrick Bird. We looked at his picture, his face smiling out from the front pages of our newspapers or our television screens, and looked at the life of this slightly unassuming man and were surprised. Derrick Bird: nice, affable, friendly, neighbourly, we kept being told. A father, a grandfather even, a doting son, a family man: a person with interests and hobbies, a man who gave to charity and went on holidays abroad. We looked at his face, we read the endless words about him and we scratched our heads because this wasn't the portrait of a killer.

Derrick Bird wasn't a loner or an oddball; he didn't hide himself away or live in a community where nobody knew him. He didn't keep himself to himself. He was a friend, a neighbour, a colleague and he came from a good family. And this is precisely why we were so shocked by it all. It wasn't just the fact that he had killed, and killed so many people at that, in such a violent and cold-blooded way. It was the fact that *he* had done it. Derrick Bird: agreeable, acceptable, kind, neighbourly. And above all ordinary.

What we didn't see behind the smile was the hidden turmoil. The anxiety that was eating away it him, the terrible insecurities he suffered from, the financial worries that he was going through and must have haunted him in the dead of the night, the terror and the shame he felt at the prospect of facing a jail sentence, the loneliness of his life since he'd never found a suitable close companion. And we didn't see that because he didn't want us to. Not even his own sons, his mother, his brothers or his close friends knew the full extent of what was going through Derrick Bird's mind. He kept his problems hidden away and they would only fully emerge on his death, and this is why we were so shocked by his actions.

Only now, with the benefit of hindsight, can we start to make some semblance of sense of it all.

In examining the profiles of spree killers psychologists frequently describe the minds of these people as being like pressure cookers waiting to go off, and this very much seems to apply to Derrick Bird.

As we have learned, Bob Cullen, who holidayed with Bird in Croatia in September of 2009, said that when drunk, Bird had spoken of taking a gun and shooting 'them all', although it is not clear to as to who Bird was referring to. Did he mean his travelling companions or was he simply using the pronoun in general? Karen Williams, the prostitute who allegedly slept with Bird in the autumn of 2005, said that he had spoken of his hatred for both his brother and the people who lived in his village, and that he told her when he 'shoots' them he'd 'know which ones they were'. Did Bird really plan a massacre as far back as five years ago? Had he been thinking about it on holiday in Croatia nine months before? Was it that premeditated or were these simply empty, drunken threats? We will never really know the answer to that because Derrick Bird took those secrets to his woodland resting place.

But even if Bird had harboured deadly thoughts for all that time he didn't act on them. For all the resentment and sibling envy he felt and the financial pressure he was under, for a time he carried on as usual – driving his cab, seeing his sons, having tea with his mother, larking around with his twin in car-based sports, attending his diving club, socialising at the pub, keeping in contact with his Thai 'girlfriend'.

Some people have said that Derrick Bird 'lost control',

but as he drove around West Cumbria on his deadly rampage, gun in hand, taking out the lives of others as and when he saw fit, for the first time in many months Bird must have felt that he finally was in control. He was the one who was in charge. The one who could decide who would live and who would die. He knew who he wanted to kill: his twin brother, his lawyer, his colleague, and some of his fellow cab drivers. And he knew the ones he would spare. Despite being in the vicinity he didn't go to his brother Brian's house, where he knew his mother would be. He would have passed the door of Linda Mills's house in Lamplugh when he killed his brother David but he didn't knock there.

And even when Bird started taking aim randomly, killing strangers, there were some people he ignored. He would take aim at teenagers but he never once aimed his gun at a child. He had looked nine-year-old Jordan Williams in the eye in Seascale having just murdered Michael Pike, but he didn't pull the trigger on him or his sister Mia, even though he had the chance. And when confronted with some of the last people to see him alive – the Tucker family – who came to assist him when he crashed in the woodland of the National Park, he took one look at mother Zoe standing there as her small sons played behind her and simply said: 'You're all right.'

The Reverend Marshall has spoken of there being two Derrick Birds. The one that people had known and loved for 52 years and the 'new' Derrick Bird that emerged from his door on the morning of 2 June: the 'stranger'. And in many ways he is right. We will never really properly know what it was that caused this man's switch to flick that morning but we can see now why it did. No one could ever condone what Derrick Bird did on that tragic day but perhaps we can begin to understand why he acted in the way that he did.

CHAPTER TWELVE

A s shocking and as devastating as they are when they occur, spree killings are relatively uncommon in the United Kingdom. Until Derrick Bird decided to kill on that day in June there had been only two spree killings on these shores in the past three decades but around the world they seem to happen all too frequently. From the United States to Australasia, from Northern Europe to the Far East they occur time and time again regardless of the country's laws, culture or economy. They are just as likely to take place in rural communities as they are capital cities, and be perpetrated by those with the benefit of wealth and education as they are by the disenfranchised. The profile of the spree killer is as varied as the location in which he chooses to kill, and the motive that drives him to do it. And it also seems reasonable to refer to 'he' and 'him' when commenting on this particular type of offender, because according to the high-profile cases so far, spree killers appear to be predominantly, if not exclusively, male.

To illustrate the above points one only has to look at three spree killings which took place between June 2001 and October of the following year. On 1 June 2001 Dipendra Bir Bikram Shah, then the Crown Prince of Nepal, shot and killed several members of his family whilst they were having dinner at the Royal Palace. Despite being well educated – he attended Eton before taking a place at Tribhuvan University in Nepal – and being extremely wealthy, Dipendra was frustrated by his family and his position. It was said that one of the motives for the killings was that he hadn't been allowed to marry the woman he wanted, and so sought vengeance on the people he believed stood in his way, shooting the family party at point-blank range. During the course of his spree he would kill ten of his family, including his parents, and injure five more before turning the gun on himself. He survived for three days in a coma, during which, thanks to a gruesome twist of logic, he held the title of 'King' as a result of his father's death.

Four months later on 27 September 2001 Friedrich Heinz Leibacher, an unemployed 57-year-old Swiss man, walked into the Zug Canton Parliament, in Switzerland, disguised as a policeman. Armed with a pump-action shotgun, a rifle and a pistol, on entering the chamber Leibacher opened fire, killing 14 members of parliament and injuring a further 18.

Leibacher, who had a both a criminal record for fraud and obscenity and had been diagnosed with a personality disorder, believed that he was the target of a government conspiracy. As such Leibacher wanted to avenge what he described as the 'Zug mafia'.

Then in October 2002 two men – John Allen Muhammed, 48, and 17-year-old Lee Boyd Malvo – would bring Washington DC to its knees when they embarked on a three-week killing spree, murdering ten people in random sniper attacks. Within the first 27 hours of their rampage they had murdered six people. Jamaican national Malvo had known a childhood defined by poverty, and he looked on Muhammed as a father figure. Although no clear motive for the killings has ever been established it is understood that Muhammed told Malvo he wanted to hold the US Government to ransom for the sum of $10 million, and that when they had obtained this money he would use it to establish a community for black homeless children in Canada. Malvo and Muhammed were eventually caught. Muhammed was later executed, whilst his accomplice is serving a life sentence for his crimes.

These were three very different cases, with four very different killers, yet the pattern was always the same.

Of all the spree killings that have happened in recent years across the world the one that resonates with most people today is that of the Columbine Massacre, which occurred in Colorado in the United States in 1999. The reason why we remember this isn't just for the ferocity of the attack itself, the fact that 13 innocent lives were taken that day, or even that it took place within the walls of a High School. It is most memorable because it was carried out by two teenage students, Eric Harris and Dylan Klebold, who were just 18 and 17 years old respectively at the time.

On the morning of 20 April the two boys, both heavily armed and wearing balaclavas and trench coats, entered the establishment and terrorised the school for an hour as they seemingly indiscriminately opened fire on their classmates and teachers alike. Not only were they carrying automatic weapons but Harris and Klebold had planted and carried with them a series of home-made bombs, which they had planned to detonate during their rampage. Fortunately, few of these would go off, but before lunchtime 12 students and one teacher would die, with a further 23 seriously wounded in the attack. Later that morning, as the FBI and specialist firearms teams surrounded the school and held the building under siege, Harris and Klebold took their lives, shooting themselves whilst in the school library, where only a short time earlier they had shot and wounded others.

Even though it was not the first attack to take place in a US school – prior to Columbine there had been a spate of gun crime occurring at High Schools across the country – this was the most violent and deadly to date, and it left America, and the rest of the world, reeling. The fact that the massacre was one of the first spree killings to unfold on live television made the ordeal all the more chilling. For few can forget the terrifying images of students fleeing from the building, and the emotional scenes of parents arriving at the school gates desperately waiting for news of their children's welfare.

But there was another reason why people were so shocked about the events that day and this was the fact that no one could understand why it had happened within this particular community. The suburb of Littleton had always been regarded as affluent, was by and large middle class, and was said to be 'close-knit'. Furthermore, both Harris and Klebold came from good families. Harris was the son of an Air Force pilot, whilst Klebold's father was a geophysicist and also ran a successful mortgage business. Both boys had shown promise at junior school. Klebold was intellectually bright and was part of a gifted students' programme while Harris was said to be a strong student and was good at soccer. However, having become friends in the ninth grade, as they grew older both Harris and Klebold seemed to change.

Bound by a mutual hatred of the 'jock' culture (a 'jock' represents the college in sporting and athletic events, and enjoys the attendant status and accolade) that was ever present at the school, and with their inability to fit in with the majority, Harris and Klebold withdrew from their fellow classmates. They started dressing differently and became part of what was known at the school as the 'Trench Coat mafia', a fringe social clique that were not only defined by their trademark long coats, dark clothes and boots, but also by the fact they liked to talk about guns and weaponry. Harris and Klebold also shared a passion with anything to do with Germany. Both were studying the language and had a fascination with Adolf Hitler, and were said by students to not only wear swastikas but to exchange Nazi salutes. They were also drawn together by their love of violent video games and music, which often had dark satanic themes and lyrics.

It was during this time that the boys, who had both previously had good conduct reports from the school, began to get into trouble. Harris was known to have violent flare-ups and on one occasion threw a ball at a friend's car windscreen in a fit of anger. In 1998 they were both arrested after stealing items from a van they broke into. As it was their first offence they were enrolled in a community service programme and had to undergo counselling, only to be released a month early on the grounds of good behaviour.

If Harris's and Klebold's parents and teachers thought they were simply going through a phase that would be understandable, for despite their change in looks, their fondness for violent video games, and their scrape with the law, on the face of it they weren't that different from a lot of their peers, who either felt alienated at school, wanted to make some kind of statement, or simply felt the need to rebel. It was only after the massacre when a full investigation began that a full, if slightly sinister, picture begin to emerge of what was really going through the teenagers' minds in the run-up to 20 April.

Amongst their possessions – their diaries, numerous writings, information on the computer hard drives, as well as messages they had left on websites – investigators were disturbed to discover not just a profile of two men in psychological free fall (Klebold spoke of suicide in his diaries, whilst on a website Harris threatened to kill anyone who had slighted him). Most chilling of all was the fact that the pair had been planning the attack for over a year. Harris had written about their plot in his diary and they had even made video tapes in which they discussed the siege.

This was no snap decision on their part, no flashpoint following a row at school or an argument with their parents. 'Judgement Day', as they had referred to it, had been planned meticulously and they had even earmarked a specific day for it to take place: 20 April, Adolf Hitler's birthday. They had gone to great lengths to obtain their weapons, relying on older friends to help them get the guns they used in the attack. And they had even learned how to make home-made bombs.

And if this wasn't disturbing enough in itself there was the realisation that Harris and Klebold hadn't planned to kill just 13 people that day. When it later emerged that they had planted a bomb in the school cafeteria it was clear they had wanted to claim hundreds of lives. They had hoped that when this explosion detonated their fellow pupils would evacuate the building, fleeing into the car park, and it was there that they planned to carry out the shootings. Luckily the bomb failed to go off, but this didn't stop them from killing and specifically targeting those they had issues with: the 'jocks' they loathed, as well as fellow students who came from ethnic minorities.

America reeled from the events at Columbine. Parents, educational authorities and the state alike would ask how and why such an atrocity could happen within their schools and would question many aspects of the case from student safety to identifying and dealing with potentially violent children. And it would also lead to Al Gore, then Vice President of the US, to back a bill to tighten the existing gun laws in the country. The bill was thrown out by Congress and the issue, which seemed to divide the US in two, was so controversial that it would become the subject of director Michael Moore's 2002 documentary *Bowling for Columbine.*

Feelings of rejection and social alienation are often commonplace in the spree killer's psyche and with Harris and Klebold this was certainly the case. Both felt that they were outsiders, both had trouble fitting in and we know that both of them had felt rejected in some way. From his diaries investigators learnt that Klebold was unhappy with the fact that he couldn't form a relationship with a member of the opposite sex. For Harris his rage with the world may have been further fuelled by the fact that his application to the US Marine Corps had been turned down.

Columbine was one of the worst school shootings ever to take place, which is why it remains in our consciousness. But just as it wasn't the first (in the run-up to Columbine a total of 16 pupils and teachers had been fatally wounded in school shootings) it wasn't the last either. Over the years there have been a number of copycat rampages where students have tried to emulate Harris's and Klebold's spree.

On 26 April 2002, 18 people were killed when 19-year-old Robert Steinhauser went on a killing spree at his former school, from which he had been expelled. This was the Gutenberg Gymnasium, in Erfurt, Germany. In the course of this rampage Steinhauser, who was dressed as a ninja, killed 13 teachers, plus another two college students and a policeman who tried to apprehend him. He then committed suicide.

In March 2005 16-year-old Jeff Weise opened fire on his classmate at the Red Lake Senior High School in Minnesota, killing five students and two members of staff. He had started his spree by firstly shooting his grandfather and then his partner to death.

Then in November 2007 Pekka-Eric Auvinen, then 18, killed his principal and seven students at Jokela High School, in Tuusula, in Finland, before shooting himself. He had posted a video on YouTube before the killings, in which he proclaimed that he wanted to 'eliminate all who I see unfit'. In the clip he is seen holding a shotgun and wearing a T-shirt printed with the slogan 'Humanity is Overrated'.

Combined feelings of rejection and isolation are emotions we see time and time again in the mindset of the spree killer. And it would appear to be this that drove 25-year-old Marc Lepine to stage one of the most brutal mass killings Canada has ever seen, when in Montreal in 1989 he shot to death 14 people in the space of one afternoon – all of them women.

On the face it Lepine didn't look or act like he was a potential threat to society. By all accounts the man who was responsible for this spree killing was quiet, well spoken, thoughtful and intelligent. However, few people ever really knew the man responsible for the atrocities at the University of Montreal, because he wasn't close to anyone; he was yet another figure who seemed to 'keep himself to himself'.

Born in Montreal in 1964, Lepine, whose original name was Gamil Gharbi, didn't have the easiest of childhoods. Eventually his parents' relationship floundered and they went their separate ways and later Gharbi would change his name, taking that of his mother's family: Lepine.

Whether it was to do with his childhood or simply just because of his personality Lepine always found it difficult to fit in, even as a young boy. Though he was bright and articulate he is said to have found it hard to make friends easily and that he was lacking in social skills. As he grew older Lepine, who had a fascination with electronics and loved war movies, had problems forming relationships with women.

According to press reports that surfaced following the killings, after leaving school Lepine applied to enter the military but his application was eventually rejected on the grounds that they believed him to be antisocial. So instead Lepine set his sights on furthering his education and gaining a place at the École Polytechnique, the engineering school at the University of Montreal. And yet despite his intellect and his aptitude for the subject Lepine was struggling with the entrance requirements he needed for the course. And even though he had enrolled in evening classes to help with his admission he found it difficult to keep up.

Frustrated by his life and his inability to achieve what he wanted, unhappy and alone, Lepine's mood darkened. In the winter of 1989 he walked into a local armament store and legitimately purchased a hunting rifle. One week later Lepine would carry out his massacre.

On the afternoon of 6 December Lepine calmly entered the buildings of the École Polytechnique, where students were celebrating the last day of term before their winter break, and began his rampage. According to several witness reports, as Lepine walked down a corridor he would shoot and kill a female member of staff before entering a lecture room, rifle in hand, where he ordered all the men in the class outside. As they evacuated the class he is then reported to have said, 'I want the women. You are all feminists.' He then proceeded to shoot at the female members of the class. In the space of just ten minutes Lepine killed 14 women and injured a further 13 people before he shot himself dead.

In a suicide note that was found after the shootings Lepine had apparently blamed feminists for ruining his life. Just like Harris and Klebold – who as stated previously had aimed and shot at the 'jocks' they loathed, as well as pupils from ethnic minorities, whom they despised for their colour alone

– Lepine had a target in mind when he went on his spree: the opposite sex. But by carrying out the massacre at the university from which he felt excluded, he was also taking a shot against the institution itself, which, to him, symbolised the rejection he felt.

Even though the detectives and psychologists who investigated the case had been given a motive for the killings in the form of a suicide note they were still left perplexed. They couldn't understand what led him to kill in such a cold and calculating way, singling out his victims simply because of their gender alone. The fact that Lepine had never shown any signs of mental instability or violent aggression before that moment baffled them even more. The case would lead to yet another country's government having to reassess their gun laws.

Tragically this would be a debate that has echoed time and time again across the world and in 1997 it was one that was heard in Australia following what would subsequently come to be known as the Port Arthur Massacre.

On 28 April 1996 Michael Bryant, then aged 30 and living in Tasmania, killed 35 people and injured another 21 in the wake of his rampage, all within a period of 24 hours.

Like Harris, Klebold and Lepine, Bryant had always been something of an outsider, although he did not possess the intellect of the other three killers. As a young child Bryant was diagnosed as having a low IQ and as such would qualify for a disability allowance when he left school. He is also said to have had difficulties in forming friendships.

On leaving school Bryant, with few options ahead of him, found work as a handyman and took a job with a family friend, Helen Harvey. The pair are said to have formed a close friendship, one that was so intense that some questioned the nature of their relationship. On Harvey's death in a car crash in 1993 (Bryant was a passenger), she left him her entire estate. Having inherited this fortune Bryant was able to live in style. He gave up work and moved into a large house in Hobart, but his new neighbours didn't warm to him and were wary of his eccentric behaviour. He is said to have kept antisocial hours, sleeping all day and walking the streets at night, and would threaten to 'kill' any of them if he thought they were trespassing on his land. As well as the luxuries he could now afford Bryant also used the money he inherited from Helen Harvey to buy himself an AK-10 semiautomatic rifle.

Of the 35 people Bryant killed on 28 April only two were known to him and they were a couple called the Martins, proprietors of a small guesthouse called 'Seascape' in the area. Bryant is said to have wanted to seek revenge on the couple because he believed that they had played a part in the suicide of his father, who had been keen to purchase a farm that the Martins had owned. The couple had allegedly 'treated his family badly', and he held a grudge against them.

Though facts are still hazy as to how Bryant's rampage started it is believed that he drove to the guesthouse in the early hours of the morning and killed the Martins before returning home. Having stocked up on ammunition and packed two rifles into a sports bag, he drove to Port Arthur where he carried out the second phase of his rampage amongst the prison ruins, which were a popular tourists' attraction.

Entering the Broken Arrow Café, which that morning was filled with tourists enjoying refreshments, he systematically shot 20 of them before heading out into the car park. He went on to kill another 11 people as he left the site – including a young mother, her six-year-old child and her toddler. At a petrol station he shot at a passing car, then took the driver of another car hostage, bundling him into the boot of his vehicle. He then returned to Seascape (the scene of his first murders), taking his hostage into the guesthouse with him, after setting fire to the car.

The police caught up with Bryant and over 200 officers surrounded the property and desperately tried to negotiate with the killer. But communications broke down that evening and the following morning Bryant set the fire to the guesthouse. Bryant fled the fire, only to be captured. However the police would later find three more bodies in the house – those of the Martins and the hostage – taking the death toll to 35. Bryant is currently serving a life sentence in a high security prison in Tasmania but has made several suicide bids over the years.

It is the apparent randomness of spree killings that seems to baffle and shock but in the majority of these cases the killer will have certain specific targets in mind before they embark on killing strangers. When Eric Borel, a 16-year-old from Toulon in France, went about his deadly spree in September 1995, the teenager began his massacre at the family home. He killed his mother, his stepfather and his half-brother before turning his gun on locals in the streets in the village of Cuers.

Although Borel is said to have been a gifted and happy student at the lycée he attended in Toulon, things were not so happy on the home front and his relationship with both his mother and his stepfather was said to be tense. Borel was the product of a brief liaison between Marie-Jeanne Parenti and Jacques Borel, who both worked in the military. When the couple drifted apart he was sent to live with his paternal grandparents, whom he was said to adore. At the age of five, much to his distress, his mother, now in a relationship with Yves Bichet, decided that she wanted him back and took him to live with them. Borel found it difficult to adjust to his new circumstances and had trouble bonding with his mother, and his relationship with Bichet was no better. Some reports have alleged that they could be strict with Borel and would frequently punish him, although some members of the Bichet family have since disputed this. Nevertheless, Borel never seemed to settle at home.

He had friends at school, his closest being Alan Guillemette whom he would spend his free time with. Otherwise he kept himself busy with his interests: tending to his chickens, taking walks and shooting small birds in the woodlands – this is a common pursuit in this part of France. Borel was also keen on anything to do with the military. He liked weapons and often spoke of his desire to join the army after school and follow in the footsteps of his father.

Although he was quiet and reserved by nature in the run-up to the killings teachers and school friends noticed a change in Borel. He confided in friends that he could no longer stand things at home; he was tired of being ordered around by his parents and longed to move away. He is alleged to have told one of his peers that he had even contemplated suicide. He also started to behave badly in class, playing truant and answering teachers back. A teacher said afterwards that the school's procedure in dealing with either troubled or problematic pupils was to send them to a social worker, but no one had thought this necessary in the case of Borel. However, while this was out of character members of staff assumed that Borel − like Harris and Klebold − was simply going through a rebellious stage, brought on by adolescence.

But, of course, it was more than just a phase. For on the evening of 23 September he shot his stepfather to death in the kitchen of their home, using a .22 calibre rifle. He then took aim at his 11-year-old half-brother who was in the living room, shooting him dead as the boy watched television. Then he bludgeoned both family members with a hammer. When his mother returned home from church that evening he killed her too, with a single shot to the head. Borel then cleaned the house and covered the bodies of his family with sheets, before shutting and locking the doors. It would be well past midnight before the crime scene was discovered by Borel's stepbrother, but by then the teenager was hiding out in the woodland, carrying his stepfather's gun, a supply of ammunition, and enough food to last him until daybreak. No one would realise Borel was missing until half-past-three in the morning.

On 24 September at around 7.30am Borel arrived at the home of his friend Alan Guillemette. The latter was still asleep but Borel asked Alan's mother to wake him. Borel waited for his companion in the garden and when the other boy came outside they are said to have had a long conversation. Though no one is certain of what they actually discussed that morning it appeared that Borel was asking Guillemette for something. But his friend seemed to refuse the request and turned to enter the house again, at which point Borel raised his rifle and shot him. Alan Guillemette died as he was airlifted to hospital.

Borel strode into the village, rifle in hand. The fact that he was carrying a gun wouldn't have raised eyebrows initially. It was the hunting season and it was common to see a boy of Borel's age going off shooting at the weekend. But this character didn't have sparrows or pigeons in his sights. He was out to kill people, as they would soon discover as he set about the final phase of his spree: shooting at random around the village of Cuers. Some would be killed on the streets, in a parking lot, in the town square, outside a bank; others would be despatched through their open windows as they went about their business in their homes. Of the victims Borel shot that day, one was a father of five, two were pensioners and his youngest victim was a teenage boy who had simply stepped out of his house to buy a loaf of bread. At the age of 17 this poor victim was just a year older than his killer.

But by 8am the game was up and, with the alarm raised and now surrounded by police, Borel, who in the course of the spree claimed the lives of 15 people, committed suicide under a cypress tree.

In the United States, following the Columbine tragedy the American authorities would come together to discuss what preventative measures could be put in place to stop a repeat of such a crime ever happening again within one of their educational establishments. Aside from the gun law debate, security at schools across the States would come under review and would be tightened and improved as a result of the massacre. Crisis strategies and management were also examined in the event that another spree killing should ever take place within a school. But the main area that was discussed at the time was how teachers and people with positions of authority working within the schools could identify and deal with potentially dangerous students.

The message was clear. America never wanted another repeat of what happened on that day in Colorado. But on 16 April 2007, nearly eight years to the day after the massacre at Columbine, America would bear witness to one of the worst mass murders in its history and once again it would take place at an educational establishment. Although this time the massacre wouldn't happen at a school but at a college, when Seung-hui Cho, a 23-year-old undergraduate at Virginia Tech University, would stage a killing spree across its campus, killing 30 people in the process.

Born in South Korea in 1984 Cho had moved to the US with his parents when he was eight years old. His family, who ran a dry-cleaning business, had been in search of a better life for their son and believed that he would benefit from an American education. But while Cho was bright, excelling in maths, and enjoyed playing basketball, he never really fitted in with his peers and from a young age was a loner. Bullied at school, Cho had few friends. As he grew older he would become increasingly introverted.

Following his graduation Cho enrolled at Virginia Tech in 2003 but once again he found it difficult to make friends. Described by college peers as being sullen and aloof he spent most of his time on his own and rarely interacted with other students on his course or within his dormitory. His lecturers also found Cho difficult to deal with. He would come to class wearing sunglasses and a baseball cap pulled down over his face and very rarely spoke even when questioned in class. During one of his first classes at the college Cho was asked to introduce himself to the group. Rather than give his name, like the other students had done, he simply held up a piece of paper. On it was written 'Question Mark'. 'That's what we called him after that,' a student said. '"The Question Mark boy". No one knew him, he never spoke. He just kept away from everyone.'

Studying English literature in his senior year Cho's

professors found his writing to be dark and often gruesome. However there were other indicators to suggest that Cho wasn't of sound mind. In 2005 he was accused of stalking two female students on the campus. That same year, following a suicidal statement he made to a fellow dormitory mate, Cho was admitted to a psychiatric hospital, where he was diagnosed with a depressive disorder. Cho was released shortly afterwards, but only on condition that he attended regular therapy sessions.

It is clear that both his peers and his professors found Cho's behaviour and demeanour to be disturbing but little was done to monitor the student and he kept himself to himself and rarely spoke to anyone. It was revealed afterwards that he suffered from selective mutism, a condition which renders a speaking person mute in social situations. Consequently, few could have known what was going on in his head, or of his deadly intent.

Cho had in fact been planning his assault on Virginia Tech for some time, as evidence would later reveal. A month before the massacre he would legally purchase his first handgun, only to procure a second only days before the attack.

On the morning of 16 April Cho awoke early and began his killing spree at 7am, killing two students in a dormitory in a hall of residence before returning to his room. Here he changed out of his bloodstained clothes, re-armed himself and then put together a package of computer files, digital photographs and film footage and documents, which he addressed to the NBC News network. At just before a quarter to ten Cho left his room, strolled out onto the campus and posted the package in a mailbox.

He then calmly strode over to a faculty building, where he had once taken a sociology class, and, in the space of just under 10 minutes, he shot and killed 30 people and injured a further 25. On discovery of the two bodies in the dormitory room the alarm had already been raised amongst the campus and local police forces. But by the time they caught up with Cho, at just before 10am, the rampage was already over. Having taken the lives of so many young people that morning, Cho committed suicide, shooting himself in the temple.

Two days after the murders NBC received Cho's package in the post. At first they were baffled as to who it had been sent from. It was only when they started examining its contents that they realised it had been sent by the 'Virginia Tech Gunman'. The package contained a long and rambling diatribe, numerous writings, 43 photographs and 28 film clips that showed Cho posing with his weapons and venting his anger against the world. In one clip he talked about being bullied and picked on by his contemporaries and of his hatred for the 'rich kids', 'brats' and 'snobs' who had 'raped his soul'. They had 'forced' him to do what he did, he said. In another film he compared himself to Jesus Christ, 'inspiring generations of the weak and the defenceless'. And, perhaps most chillingly of all, Cho paid homage to the perpetrators of other massacres, singling out the Columbine killers Eric Harris and Dylan Klebold, whom he described as 'martyrs'.

Cho, the silent boy whom no one could get a word out of in life, had finally found his voice in death.

CHAPTER THIRTEEN

When news first began to break about the extent of Derrick Bird's rampage across West Cumbria it was almost impossible not to cast one's mind back to the last two spree killings that took place in the United Kingdom, and the names of their perpetrators. These are Michael Ryan, who in 1987 wreaked carnage in the streets of Hungerford, in Berkshire, England, and Thomas Hamilton, who would stage a deadly spree in the Scottish town of Dunblane nearly a decade later.

It was inevitable that we should think of these because before the events of 2 June these were the two most atrocious examples of mass murder involving firearms in the history of the British Isles. In Hungerford Michael Ryan would kill 16 people, including his own mother. In Dunblane Thomas Hamilton would take the lives of 16 children and one adult in a spree that lasted less than three minutes. Both incidents would shock the nation, both crimes would shatter their respective communities and both would result in the repeal of the gun laws in the United Kingdom.

But there was another reason why it was only natural that comparisons would be drawn between Hungerford and Dunblane and the events in West Cumbria. This was that all three spree killings took place in rural settings, in towns and villages where the crime rate was normally low. They hadn't occurred in London, Manchester or Glasgow but in places which are invariably are described as 'sleepy', 'picturesque', 'peaceful' and amongst communities which are said to be 'close-knit', 'friendly' and 'welcoming'.

Certainly this can be said of Hungerford, a pretty and friendly market town, in the heart of Berkshire. It has a historic marketplace, many antique shops that line the High Street, stalls that fill its arcade, pubs, restaurants and tea rooms; you can take towpath walks along its canal and the local River Kennet is beautiful. So it is little wonder that Hungerford has long been regarded as one of the most attractive market towns in England.

But on a warm and sunny afternoon in August 1987 all that was good about Hungerford was to be forgotten when Michael Ryan, an unemployed 27-year-old from the area, decided to stage a war on the town and its people for no apparent reason.

Michael Ryan was an unemployed labourer and sometime antiques dealer. Born in Marlborough, Wiltshire, he was an only child. His father was 55 years old when Ryan came into the world and died two years before the killings. This future killer was described by some as being something of a 'mummy's boy', which was largely to do with the fact that at 27 he was still living at home.

Ryan had an obsessive fascination with firearms. Not only did he subscribe to a number of magazines specialising in weaponry as well as survival skills, such as *Soldier of Fortune*, but he was a great fan of action films such at Sylvester Stallone's *Rambo* productions.

Just like Derrick Bird, Michael Ryan possessed gun licences and – these being more lenient times before the laws were tightened as a result of his actions – he had in his possession at the time of the killings two shotguns, two semiautomatic pistols and two semiautomatic rifles, all of which he was legally allowed to own.

On the day of the massacre he would not only kill 16 people but he would seriously wound another 15. His rampage would begin on 19 August in the Savernake Forest, an area of woodland several miles west of Hungerford. At approximately 12.30pm he came across a 35-year-old woman out picnicking with her two young children. Approaching her, he ordered the mother at gunpoint to put her children in the car before he walked her back into the woods and shot her 13 times in the back. The police would first be alerted to this dreadful event when a pensioner was stopped by the children to say that a man had 'shot mummy'.

Heading back to his mother's house in Southview on the outskirts of the town Ryan stopped at a petrol station, filled his car with petrol and shot at the cashier. Back at home he entered the house to stock up on weapons and ammunition and got back into his car. When it didn't start, the frustrated murderer shot at the vehicle before re-entering the house, shooting his mother's pet dog and then setting fire to the property. He then armed himself with the weaponry he had previously loaded in the boot of his car, and walked out into the street and killed his neighbours, who were out in their garden.

It was in Southview that Ryan killed his mother. On seeing her son armed, her house on fire, and people lying dead, she confronted the 27-year-old and pleaded with him to stop. But Ryan simply ignored her and shot her dead.

He then calmly proceeded on foot – shooting, injuring and killing along his journey. As he made his way into the centre of town Ryan, who was dressed in combat gear and heavily armed, fired indiscriminately. Amongst his victims were motorists who came across his path, neighbours from Southview, the townspeople of Hungerford out doing their daily business, and a local policeman who had arrived in the road to investigate reports of gunfire.

The scenes across Hungerford that day where chaotic to say the least. In an era when few people possessed mobile phones it was difficult for anyone to know what was going on, let alone warn each other to stay away from the crime scene or out of Ryan's path. Reports would filter through that there was a gunman on the loose, that gunfire and sirens had been heard, cars had crashed, and bodies lay strewn over the streets. But still no one really knew what was happening. All they knew was that Hungerford, this once peaceful and genteel town, was now not only a scene of carnage, but was under siege.

The police were in pursuit of Ryan but for much of the afternoon he was to evade capture. Having shot and killed 16 people, seriously injuring 15, as well as maiming many more, Ryan then broke into the John O'Gaunt School on the outskirts of town, where he had once been a student. Michael Ryan barricaded himself in a classroom. Police surrounded the building, and helicopters – which had tried to follow his movements when he was on foot – circled above, and negotiators desperately tried to make contact; but the attempt at mediation failed. Ryan was not in the mood to co-operate, let alone give himself up.

The rampage, which had lasted for nearly seven hours, finally came to an end at 6.52pm, when Ryan took his own life, shooting himself in the head. According to many subsequent reports that followed, his parting shot to negotiators who were trying to reason with him was said to have been: 'Hungerford must be a bit of a mess. I wish I'd stayed in bed.'

At the time the Hungerford Massacre had been Britain's worst mass killing and for nearly a decade it would remain that way. However on 13 March 1996 that was to change, because on that day Thomas Hamilton, a 43-year-old former shopkeeper, would single-handedly cause one of the most horrific mass killings not just in the history of the British Isles, but in the world. Because when Hamilton went about his deadly spree his chosen targets were children.

Dunblane is a small and picturesque cathedral city that lies north of Stirling, in Scotland. Though it is often referred to as a city because of its cathedral its population is relatively small and as such it has more of the feel of a town, for this is place where everyone knows everyone else. Families have lived here for generations, never finding either the desire or the need to move anywhere else, and there is a strong sense of community spirit amongst its people. In recent years Dunblane has expanded and it is easy to understand why so many people from the surrounding area would want to live there. For aside from the attractions of the town centre itself – the cathedral, the historic buildings in the old town, its bustling high street and the Allan Water that runs through it – accessible road and rail links to Stirling, Glasgow, Edinburgh and Perth put it within the commuter belt of all of these cities.

But there is another reason why so many young families have chosen to make Dunblane their home: this lovely town boasts some of the best schools in the whole of Scotland, both at primary and secondary level. And so the fact that Britain's second most deadly mass murder should take place not just in Dunblane, but within the walls of one its primary schools, made the atrocity all the more repugnant. None of the residents of Dunblane could ever have imagined that such a crime would take place in their school grounds, not least the parents who had waved their little ones off as they headed into Dunblane Primary that morning.

Whilst numerous motives have been given for Thomas Hamilton's actions that day one can't even begin to imagine what was going through his head as he made his way down the street from his house on the Kent Road to the Dunblane Primary School, on Doune Road. As John Major, the then Prime Minister, said after the attack it was, 'Such a sick and evil act, it defies comprehension.'

It was just before 9.30am when 43-year-old Hamilton arrived at the school entrance. Armed with four handguns and a pair of pliers he first cut the school's telephone wires (accessible on a nearby pole) before entering through the gates. The school day was already underway and the children were attending the first class of the morning. Hamilton, who was wearing a khaki-coloured top and a pair of ear-muffs (for silencing the sound of the gunfire) then strode into the playground and into the school building. Making his way down a corridor he threw open the door of the gymnasium, where three teachers were taking a PE class with a group of five- to six-year-olds.

Without a moment's hesitation the gunman fired at and injured two teachers, before opening up at the children, discharging over 100 rounds in less than three minutes. All three teachers desperately tried to shield their pupils from his fire, trying to usher some of them to the safety in a store cupboard. However, tragically there was only so much they could do and within that short space of time Hamilton would take the lives of 16 innocent and defenceless children and their teacher Gwen Mayor, as well as seriously injuring many more in the process.

Hamilton then left the gymnasium, walked down a corridor of classrooms and made his way back to the playground, where he started taking aim at a mobile schoolroom. But having heard the gunshots and realising that there was something wrong, the quick-thinking teacher had already instructed her pupils to take cover under their desks and chairs and had barricaded the door. Her swift response saved their lives for, although the bullets hit books and school equipment, the children were left unscathed.

Thwarted in his plans to take further lives Hamilton returned to the gymnasium and, using one of the two revolvers pointed at his mouth, pulled the trigger and killed himself. When the police and paramedics entered the building shortly afterwards they found scenes of such indescribable carnage that, to this day, few have been able to excise them from their minds.

What these spree killings have in common with the events in Cumbria – aside from the multiple loss of lives and the suicide of the perpetrator – is that they were not only carried out in towns which were not just attractive places to live, with low crime rates, but they were executed by men who, on the face of it, seemed quite 'normal'. Ryan was well known within the community. His father Alfred had been a government building inspector during his lifetime, whilst his mother Dorothy worked as a dinner lady at the town's primary school, before taking a job at as a waitress at a local hotel. The couple were popular and respected people and they gave their only son a good home.

Hamilton had been a shopkeeper for a time and as such would have been a well-known figure within his neighbourhood. He had also been a Scout Leader with the Stirlingshire Scout Association and he was immensely proud of this. For not only was he contributing something to society, but he held a position of responsibility, and this meant a lot to him.

But scratch a little further and other pictures emerge. Ryan, we would learn, had struggled in life and was frustrated by his own lack of achievement. He had not excelled at school and from a young age had been teased by his fellow classmates who made fun of the fact that he was short for his age. Rather than fight back Ryan avoided other children, preferring to keep his own company instead. Some family and friends later suggested that his mother – who was said to have doted on Ryan, he being her only child – spoiled him as a result and that he frequently got his own way. She would make excuses for his sullen ways and mood swings and later in life, when he couldn't find work, would bankroll him, allowing him to remain at home, meeting his car and petrol costs. She had even given him money for the purchase of his first shotgun.

At the age of 16, Ryan left the John O'Gaunt School – where he had ended his rampage and his life – and went on to technical college in order to further his education. But when it soon became clear that he was not achieving anything there he gave up on that. For the next ten years Ryan would drift aimlessly from job to job. He would work as caretaker, a labourer and at one of the antique shops in Hungerford. 'He was nice enough to say hello to but he always seemed a little lost,' a former resident of Hungerford explained. 'He just couldn't seem to find his way and that frustrated him. You could see it was eating away at him.'

Perhaps this was the reason why Ryan thought it necessary to create a fantasy life for himself. When he met people he would invariably tell them that he had a girlfriend, that he was about to open a gun shop, or even that he owned one, and that he had served in the armed forces, in the parachute corps, no less. Certainly Ryan would have enjoyed any of those occupations for he was obsessed with anything to do with warfare. He would often dress in combat clothing he bought from army surplus stores and would often be seen round the Savernake Forest in this get-up 'as though he was on patrol' one local said. Retreating into his own world Ryan became increasingly interested in weaponry. When he was old enough, and had been granted a gun licence, he started collecting firearms and would join a local gun club, where he was remembered for being an 'excellent shot'.

Today Ryan's collection of pistols, rifles – many of which were semiautomatic – and his shotguns would be regarded as an arsenal. However in 1987, prior to the subsequent revision in the gun laws, he was legitimately allowed to possess them all, having had each of his licence applications approved. However, questions were asked later as to why Ryan both wanted and needed to have so many lethal firearms in his possession. Was it the case that guns gave Ryan a sense of power and control that had otherwise eluded him in life; an empowerment which he chose to exercise on the day of the Hungerford Massacre?

In his occupation as a shopkeeper, running a local DIY store, and through his work with Scouts, you would assume that Thomas Hamilton was an affable and genial type of person: one who was liked and trusted by members of his community. But in reality nothing could have been further from the truth.

Born in Glasgow in 1952 Hamilton was raised by his grandparents, whom for many years he believed to be his natural parents. It wasn't until he was in his early twenties that he discovered that the woman he thought to be his sister was actually his real mother. If this bothered him at the time he didn't let on to anyone outside his family circle, and he would stay in contact with his birth mother throughout his adulthood.

However, it was later revealed that Hamilton had problems

bonding with women and never formed any lasting or significant relationships with the opposite sex or his own. Instead what time he had when away from the shop was given over to his duties with the Scouts. At first he did well within the organisation. At the age of 20 he was made Assistant Scout Leader of the Stirling Division before being promoted a couple of years later to the position of Leader. However, following a series of complaints from the parents of the boys in his care, Hamilton's role within the organisation was subject to an inquiry and he would later be asked for his resignation.

Of all the allegations made about Hamilton's inappropriate behaviour the most serious of all was that on two occasions he had forced the boys in his care to sleep out overnight in his sole company, rather than find suitable accommodation for the children at a hostel.

As a result of this Hamilton would have his Scout Warrant withdrawn by the County Commissioner, who questioned his 'moral intentions towards boys'. During a meeting between the two men the County Commissioner would later surmise that Hamilton 'was not of stable mind', that he suffered from 'delusions of grandeur' and that he had a 'persecution complex'. It was this last judgement that was perhaps the most insightful, for over the next two decades Hamilton seemed to wage war on all those he believed to have wronged him.

A serious bearer of grudges and an embittered malcontent, Hamilton would later claim that these 'rumours', as he called them, had resulted in the failure of his business, which later folded. He preoccupied himself with writing angry letters to numerous figures in positions of authority, including two MPs who lived in Dunblane – Michael Forsyth and George Robertson – as well as the Queen.

Despite numerous attempts to have himself reinstated within the Scout movement Hamilton failed. Blacklisted from the organisation he went on to form Boys' Clubs of his own, running his groups through a series of local schools. At first they were popular and well attended, not least the one he formed in Dunblane. However, when parents once again started to question his increasingly erratic behaviour towards their children, and attendance consequently fell, Hamilton became depressed and frustrated.

He turned his attentions instead to indulging in a hobby that he had taken up in his teens: shooting. A licensed owner of four handguns, Thomas Hamilton was an active member of his local gun club. At the time no one at the club thought anything of it, they just assumed that, like them, he simply enjoyed the sport. And they wouldn't think about it again until news broke of the terrible acts that he had carried out on the morning of 13 March 1996.

Michael Ryan and Thomas Hamilton were men who embarked upon their rampages because they were embittered by a sense of rejection, felt alienated from society, and as a result bore grudges against the world and wanted to vent their anger on the innocent. And up until the moment when

Derrick Bird stepped out of the front door of his pebble-dashed house in Rowrah and into his Citroen Picasso on that fateful morning of 2 June 2010, they were two of the most brutal killers in the history of the United Kingdom.

CHAPTER FOURTEEN

It is inevitable that in the wake of any violent crime, especially one on the scale that happened in Cumbria in June 2010, questions will follow. Whether it is from those who have been directly affected by the tragedy, the public, the media or parliament itself, people need answers. They need to know whether such ghastly events could have been prevented in any way, whether the episode was dealt with appropriately at the time, and, above all, what lessons can be learned from the tragedy.

Given the nature of the killings on 2 June it was almost par for the course that the first area of focus would be the whole subject of gun ownership and control in the country – a topic that the Prime Minister would pre-empt when he stated in his press conference at Downing Street on the day after the shootings that there should no knee-jerk reaction in response to the massacre.

But the media, the public and MPs, still wanted to address the issue and voice their concerns: they wanted to know how and why it was that Derrick Bird had been able to carry a gun licence in the first place – not just because he seemed to be of an unsound mind but because he had a criminal record. They wanted to know whether the laws in this country were tight enough and whether they should be reviewed again. And they asked whether it was the case that there were certain loopholes within our existing system that had allowed Derrick Bird to obtain his licence.

Whilst Prime Minister David Cameron conceded that an enquiry should be led into the matter he was reluctant to make any decisions relating to the killings in haste. 'The right thing to do is of course to look at all of these issues and have an open mind,' he said. 'But we should be clear that in this country we have some of the toughest gun-control legislation anywhere in the world and we should not make any knee-jerk reaction to think that there is some instant legislative or regulatory answer.'

Amongst those who called for reform was Alan Johnson, the Shadow Home Secretary, who said there should be tougher follow-up checks on gun owners, especially in regard to mental health. He said that he hoped a review on the issue would focus on whether the existing checks on licensed gun owners were thorough enough. And he questioned whether the NHS and GPs could play a greater part in the assessment process.

John Pugh, Liberal Democrat MP for Southport, went

further, wanting to know what justification there was for a 'simple taxi driver' to be in lawful possession of 'such a formidable and devastating arsenal' – a question that would be asked across the country. Home Secretary Theresa May, in response, said there would be a full Commons debate on the matter before the summer recess, after which the affair would be investigated at the highest level.

Britain does have some of the most stringent gun laws in the world. In the United States of America an individual can declare it as their constitutional right to bear arms, and people are even able to buy weapons over the counter. In the UK gun licence applicants have to undergo a long and complicated process before they are deemed fit to possess a gun. It is a lengthy procedure, one that is specifically designed to reduce the chance of anyone who is not of the right mind or character being able to get their hands on a gun. It is a system of paperwork, assessment and interviews that can take many months to complete.

In the UK an individual applying for a gun licence, as well as having two named character referees, must provide access to their medical reports and their GP. They are legally bound to disclose any criminal conviction no matter how minor, and must be prepared to be interviewed in person by the police at any time.

Furthermore, the police, who administer the gun laws in this country, are entitled to inspect the applicant's property to ensure that the weapons are stored securely, under lock and key, and each licence must be renewed every five years. Each applicant must prove to the police, who uphold the law in this instance, that they are not a danger to society in any way. Moreover, there is not one blanket licence for gun ownership. Each gun must be registered and there are separate licences for shotguns and for firearms.

In the past 25 years there have been numerous reviews of the gun laws in this country – most notably following the Hungerford massacre in 1987 and nine years later, following the events in Dunblane.

After the Hungerford killings, under the 1988 Firearms Act, there was a blanket ban on all modern semiautomatic and pump-action rifles (those that can be fired rapidly without needing to be reloaded), short rifles and self-loading rifles.

And in 1997, following Dunblane and a well supported petition led by the Snowdrop Campaign – which had been founded by friends of the bereaved families and the town's community – the laws would be amended again. Parliament, under the new Labour Government which had just come to power, passed a law prohibiting the ownership of handguns. Today anyone caught in possession of a handgun faces a mandatory five-year prison sentence.

But as stringent as our gun laws are said to be, some people have called into question whether the legislation is far-reaching enough. It is, for example, according to Home Office guidelines, not mandatory for the police to make house calls to an applicant or a current licensee. Home visits only need to be carried out if there are any concerns about the subject's medical history.

In regard to the health of an applicant, whilst the subject must allow access to their GP, Home Office guidance does make it a prerequisite, saying that any such approach 'should not be made as a matter of routine' and that it is 'impractical' for 'psychiatric assessments' to be conducted on the subject's suitability to possess any kind of gun. The fact that it is possible to renew a gun licence by post in some parts of the British Isles (Cumbria being one of these) also means that it is possible to legally own a gun for ten years without having any personal contact with the licensing officers or the police.

Given the above, it is easy to see why some believe that it's time to review our gun laws again.

The question is would the tightening of any such law have prevented what occurred on 2 June? Some say that unless there had been a complete blanket ban on the use of all guns, possibly it would have made no difference. Whilst others – within the police force, Westminster and the gun lobby – argue that such a ban could create far more serious problems in the long term. These might include a surge in the possession of illegal and even home-made weaponry, which, in the absence of licensing, the police would have no control over whatsoever.

What we do know, however, is that Derrick Bird was the legitimate and licensed owner of both a shotgun and a .22 rifle, the weapons he used during the massacre, as was confirmed by Stuart Hyde, the Deputy Chief Constable of

Cumbria Constabulary. 'He had a shotgun certificate and a firearms license for weapons,' Mr Hyde said shortly after the killings, though he refused to be drawn on whether those actual weapons had been used at the time until the ballistic report had been completed.

Bird had held a gun licence on and off for the past 20 years and at no point had his suitability to own a gun been called into question. As many as a thousand licences are revoked every year. The licence for his shotgun had been issued in 1995 and in 2007 he was granted a separate licence which allowed him to own a .22 rifle. Moreover, there are records to show that Bird, who had been granted the firearms licence for 'shooting vermin and recreational target practice' had been interviewed at home by the police at the time, and they seemed satisfied with the visit.

And even though Bird had a criminal record, for the theft at Sellafield, he was still entitled to possess a gun. According to the Home Office, people who have been sentenced for three months or more in prison are automatically banned from possessing any type of gun for at least five years. But as Bird had been given a 12-month suspended sentence for his conviction in 1990 he didn't fall into that category. He had never served time in prison, nor did he have a history of violence, which again would have counted against him. Derrick Bird, it would appear, was completely within his rights and the law to hold a gun licence.

With regard to whether Bird was either 'physically or

mentally fit' to possess a gun it's unclear what his GP's assessment was. Having received a licence for both weapons it must be assumed that it was a positive one. People have argued that Bird wasn't of a 'sound mind', but that is easy to say in retrospect. Prior to 2 June few people realised that Bird was having any problems and even if they had known about his tax difficulties, his finances, his heartbreak, his resentment towards his brother – would that have been enough to justify revoking his gun licence?

One of the questions GPs are asked to answer when gun applications are made is whether the applicant has any issue with a family member, particularly one living in the same house where the weapons and ammunition are stored. Derrick Bird lived alone and even if he did have grievances against his brother, few people were aware of it, even among his own family. Indeed there were some that didn't know that Derrick even had a twin brother.

If Bird had not been receiving psychiatric help, had not been prescribed antidepressants and had never discussed any mental issues with his doctor, they may not have regarded him as a threat, seeing him only for what he was: a slightly tubby 52-year-old, who could do with losing some weight and would be well advised to cut down on his drinking. For unless Bird presented symptoms of mental imbalance to his doctor, then there was no need for them to raise any kind of alarm with the licensing officers. Even with the application form on the GP's desk, the doctor might have thought nothing of signing it off, just as is normal practice for hundreds of patients.

This is because it is rural Cumbria, a place where gun ownership is not just commonplace but an integral part of community life. Using firearms is not just a pastime here. For the farmers, landowners, and countrymen and women who live in this region, and in other ones like it for that matter, shooting is a practical part of their lives. Here guns are not merely used for sport, but for protecting land and crops from vermin, livestock from foxes, and for other similar purposes.

When the Liberal Democrat MP John Pugh asked the House what justification was there for 'a simple taxi driver' to own such a 'formidable arsenal of weapons', it could be said that he missed the point. Derrick Bird may have been a taxi driver by trade but he was a countryman at heart and by birthright. Shooting was very much part of his life, as it is for many people who live in rural areas the length and breadth of the British Isles. As for his 'arsenal' it was not that 'formidable'. The two types of weapons in Bird's possession would be used for different purposes.

The shotgun, a long-barrelled weapon with a smooth bore, which fires no more than two cartridges before it requires reloading, is the type of weapon normally carried by gamekeepers and farmers. It is commonly used across the country for standard tasks – for instance shooting birds and for the containment of foxes. By contrast, rifles are categorised as firearms and fire bullets across a longer and more specific range. They would normally be used for shooting rabbits or stalking deer.

The criteria for obtaining a licence for a firearm is, therefore, far more stringent than for obtaining one for a shotgun, and applicants are asked what specific purpose the firearm is needed for. Derrick Bird said it was for the shooting of vermin.

Bird had been raised as a man of the country and at an early age would be taken out by his parent on shooting expeditions across the countryside. In the woodlands around Ennerdale they would shoot birds, and across the valley and the fields they would go lamping for rabbits. There was nothing uncommon or untoward in this. By teaching his sons to shoot and by taking them out with him when he went lamping, Joseph Bird wasn't breaking any rules; he was simply trying to introduce his sons to a much loved and practiced country pursuit. He was merely passing on a tradition from father to son.

Friends say they were aware that Bird was in possession of guns and say that the shotgun had been passed onto him by his father when he died. But none of them ever gave it a second thought. Even the passers-by who had seen Bird holding the shotgun when he crashed his car in the woodland of the National Park didn't think there was anything particularly untoward about it. They thought it was simply a 'common' sight for someone to witness in the area.

Bird's neighbours say that whilst they knew he liked to go out for the odd shooting expedition they had never seen him in the street with either weapon. And whilst Bird may have enjoyed spending time at the shooting range in Pattaya,

Thailand, he did so in the company of friends who had enjoyed the excursions there too. By all accounts Bird was simply a man who knew how to shoot and enjoyed it as a recreation. He may have owned two guns, but, according to friends, he was by no means a gun fanatic and there is no record of him belonging to a gun club in the UK.

It is only right that the government should review this country's gun laws once again. It is essential that the topic is fully debated in parliament and it is imperative that if there are any loopholes within the current system these should be scrutinised.

The question that still hangs it the air, however, is whether any new legislation would have stopped Derrick Bird, a man so intent on killing, from somehow fulfilling his death wish.

As David Cameron said, how do you legislate 'against a switch flicking in someone's head'? For if Derrick Bird hadn't had access to two licensed guns, would he have found another means of conducting his deadly rampage?

CHAPTER FIFTEEN

In the days that followed the killings there was a second issue that would be called into question: the role the police played on the day of the massacre. Few people like to question either the integrity or the professionalism of the police force, but following the events of 2 June there would be calls from many sections of society wanting to know how and why it was that a lone gunman was able to somehow elude the police for three hours, and carry out his rampage, killing 12 people and seriously injuring another 11 without getting caught. He was not even confronted on his murderous travels.

Questions were asked by the media. Locals wanted to know why the carnage hadn't been stopped sooner. Angry posts were sent to websites by people who simply couldn't fathom why the police seemed to fail the inhabitants of

West Cumbria on that day. How was it that Derrick Bird was able to carry out the very public 'second phase' of his killing spree without getting caught, they asked?

As details of the events of 2 June emerged, it transpired that the only time the police had actually seen Bird was in Whitehaven itself. After that, the killer was lost to them and for the next two hours he was alone on the road, free to carry out his assassinations without anyone in pursuit. How was it that the authorities were so slow to react to the events unfolding before everyone else's eyes? Why was it that Derrick Bird was able to elude them for so many hours on his 43-mile rampage?

We know that until the moment that neighbours heard shots over Frizington at 10.20am, when Bird killed Kevin Commons, the police were unaware that there was any trouble within the area. And it was not until Darren Rewcastle was gunned down in Whitehaven at around 10.33am they had any idea that they were possibly dealing with a mass murderer. But what happened thereafter? If, as some have suggested, the police had acted sooner, could the random killings of Susan Hughes, Kenneth Fishburn, Issac Dixon, Jennifer and Jimmy Jackson, Jamie Clark, Michael Pike and Jane Robinson possibly have been avoided?

Stuart Hyde, the Deputy Chief Constable for Cumbria, said it could not, asserting that the police officers chasing Bird had done everything within their power and within their call of duty to stop the gunman, attesting that at no point 'did they have the opportunity to end the killings sooner'.

'Our officers are expected to deal with difficult and challenging situations,' Mr Hyde explained. 'This incident was unprecedented, with exceptional circumstances, fast moving and highly dangerous. Had any officer or member of staff had the clear opportunity to stop Bird they would have taken it.'

Painting a picture of the events as they unfolded that day, Hyde went on to explain that the first sighting of Derrick Bird came just after 10.30am, when a local officer at the police station in Whitehaven heard gunshots coming from Duke Street. He ran out of the station on to the highway, only to be confronted by the sight of Bird in his taxi, aiming his shotgun out of the driver's side window. The officer – PC Mick Taylor – immediately alerted the station via his radio but since he was on foot, and without a vehicle, he decided to commandeer a passing vehicle to give chase.

The car, or rather cab, he took control of, an S-reg, blue Ford Escort, was driven by local man Paul Goodwin, who, despite having witnessed the events on Duke Street, was willing to assist PC Taylor. The two men then pursued Bird's Citroen Picasso along Lowther Street, before turning into Coach Road. It was at that moment that they saw Bird pull up alongside Terry Kennedy's cab and shoot him. Feeling that they had no option other than to assist Kennedy, the cab stopped and the officer administered first aid to the driver and his passenger.

At this point, alerted to the situation from the control room, a police transit van with two other officers, again unarmed, arrived on the scene and went in pursuit of Bird along Coach Street, hoping to follow him out of town. But, to their surprise, the gunman turned back on himself, pulled into a driveway along the street, stopped the car and took aim at them, his rifle clearly pointing their way. Unable to reverse because of the traffic behind them, and since they were unarmed, the officers had no choice other than to take cover. One of them sheltered under the dashboard, whilst the other tried to duck down.

'If someone points a gun or a weapon at you, you focus on the weapon,' Hyde said in defence of his officers. Quite how the two unarmed policemen could have challenged Bird at that moment is questionable as things stand. Regardless of the rules set out by the Association of Chief Police Officers, which state that when confronted with an armed assailant unarmed officers should not 'attempt to stop the vehicle but armed assistance should be sought,' faced with the business end of Bird's gun, the pair had no other option other than to take cover.

'The officers were forced to protect themselves after it became clear they could not reverse up due to the traffic build-up,' Hyde explained. 'He then drove off at speed. Despite having just witnessed a shooting and having a gun pointed at them, the officers attempted to follow him and despite asking a passer-by where he had driven, were unable to locate him again.' At a junction leading out of town Bird had headed towards a housing estate, and when the transit van made it to that point, he was already out of sight. Faced with three options the officers chose to carry on along the main road. Bird was now lost to them and, even if they had chosen the right road, the force would also later admit that the transit van, which is used to ferry prisoners, was not suitable for a high-speed chase.

This would be the last time that the police would have Bird within their vision on the road. From that point on the cab driver, with his extensive and intricate knowledge of the back roads and shorts cuts of the surrounding area, would always have been one step ahead of them, winding his way around the countryside on his deadly mission.

In the days that followed many people asked why the local police hadn't sent more officers to the scene in Whitehaven when the first shots were heard shortly after 10.30am. The answer to this appears to be that all the available patrol cars from Whitehaven had already been deployed to the Frizington area to investigate the shots heard at Kevin Commons's house. It should also be noted that at this point there was nothing to indicate to the Cumbrian police force that the two incidents were related. Bird's rampage in Whitehaven occurred within the space of just twenty very confused minutes, and it was only as numerous calls started to filter through in those first few minutes that the authorities became aware of the fact that they were dealing with a spree killer.

The Cumbrian Police Force is one of the smallest in the country. It is said to have just under 1,300 officers to police the entire county and of those officers only 42 of them are armed, all of whom are said to have been deployed on the day. As Hyde pointed out: 'These were normal neighbourhood police officers. It is completely unusual for them to have to face something like this.' What is more, the Cumbrian force do not have any helicopters at their disposal. Instead they would have to turn to the RAF and the Lancashire police force for support, which in itself took time.

Try as they did to keep up with Bird he was always ahead of them. He would have known by now that the chase was on. Not only had he been confronted by the police presence as he headed out of Whitehaven, but thanks to the information given to them by Paul Williams they now had his mobile telephone number and were calling him. But Bird was not going to pick up. He was intent in getting to the home of Jason Carey, the fourth intended victim on his list, and would drive cross-country through the villages and hamlets shooting and killing at random to get there. Without a helicopter to monitor Bird's shifting location from above, the police would be left in the dark as to where he was going, and how he was getting there.

With the alarm now raised as to who and what they were dealing with we are told that the police issued armed officers in the area with a shoot-to-kill order. The instructions were clear: if Bird came into sight they should engage and shoot if necessary.

Craig Mackey, Chief Constable of the Cumbria Police, confirmed this in a conference he would give after the event, but unfortunately, despite being only 30 seconds away from Bird towards the latter part of the spree, they were not able to carry this out. 'From what we know, at no stage did any police officer have the chance to end this any sooner,' he said, adding that that every single armed officer in the county was deployed once details of the first killings emerged.

With Bird out of their line of vision the police had to rely on emergency calls and witness reports during part of the rampage. And by all accounts it wasn't until Bird approached Seascale that officers would have him in their sights again, but even then they were hindered in their pursuit. The collision between Bird's Citroen and Harry Berger's Land Rover on the route into Seascale added valuable minutes on to their chase as police waited for the Land Rover to be moved away before they were able to pass. In the interim period Bird took the lives of two people in swift succession – those of Michael Pike and Jane Robinson.

As Derrick Bird headed out of Seascale and east towards the Lake District National Park to Eskdale Green and Boot, plans were laid down to cordon off the area. Armed units arrived, sweeping people off the streets of the local hamlets and villages and encouraging them back into their homes. All routes out of the park were sealed off and, according to one report, marksmen were dropped by helicopter at the Harknott Pass, with the objective of ambushing the killer as he drove into the village of Boot. But this was not to be, for with tyres now shredded from his collision with the stone wall on the way into the National Park, Bird was forced to come off the road and on to a woodland pass. It was here that his car crashed.

Derrick Bird continued the journey of the last few moments of his life on foot, shielded by a canopy of thick woodland from the gaze of the helicopter crew, whose craft was whirring overhead.

At 1.30pm two shots were heard, signalling the end of Bird's life and the termination of the police chase.

In the weeks that followed the Cumbrian Police Force would submit themselves and their case to the Independent Police Complaints Commission for inquiry, so that a full assessment could be given into the actions of the 100 or so officers involved in the case to see whether they handled the situation to the best of their abilities, and also to see if lessons could be learned from the incident.

Stuart Hyde was open to suggestions that the situation could have been handled differently but added: 'With hindsight, it is possible people might have believed we could have got there faster or done other things. The reality of it was that this was an exceptional incident in exceptional circumstances.'

CHAPTER SIXTEEN

No one is denying that this was, as Deputy Chief Constable Stuart Hyde described it, an 'exceptional incident, in exceptional circumstances'. When the Cumbrian community awoke on the morning of 2 June, no one could have foreseen the dreadful events that were to unfold that day. As people went about their daily business that morning – going to work, running errands or simply enjoying the sunshine – not one of them for a moment could have predicted that by lunchtime 12 members of their community would be dead.

The police started their shifts that morning – either in the station or on the road – just as on any other day. If you had told them that within the space of a couple of hours they would be not only dealing with a major incident but also trying to tackle an armed and dangerous gunman who was on the loose, they probably would have dismissed the idea and got back to their paperwork. For this is West Cumbria, a place where the crime rate is low. So low, in fact, that people think nothing of leaving their cars or their houses unlocked at night. As one resident said, 'I've never locked a door behind me in my life and I've been here for thirty years. I must know hundreds of people round here and not one of them has ever been burgled. It wouldn't feel right locking my door. It's not like being in a city. People around here know and trust each other.'

With this in mind, perhaps the criticism of the police's actions on that day has been harsh. The reality is that this was an exceptional situation. No blame can be laid at the door of the Cumbrian Police Force for the fact that they weren't well enough equipped to deal with the situation in terms of having more armed officers on the ground or even a helicopter at their disposal. These matters will in time be subject to review. And it can be said that they dealt with the incident to the best of all their abilities. The police constable who commandeered a taxi to go in pursuit of Bird in Whitehaven showed initiative. The two armed officers in the transit van who Bird aimed and shot at, but who still tried to trail him afterwards, should be commended for their bravery. For as DCC Hyde noted: 'These officers were unarmed, they [had] limited firearms awareness training and their actions were exemplary.'

And even when the armed forces were deployed and were trying to pursue Bird this was an almost impossible task. With his knowledge of the roads and the short cuts that crisscross the 43-mile radius in which he carried out his rampage, he would always be one step ahead of them. Trying to second-guess his next move was almost impossible.

There is, however, one area in which some people have criticised the police. That is the way they communicated with the other emergency services. And this, it should be noted, has not been instigated by the media or the general public, but from people who were there at the time. Critics include the witnesses, the injured and the medics who were there on the scene.

Witnesses have said that they were extremely alarmed by the length of time it took for the emergency services to come to the aid of the victims. In some cases, according to the *Independent*, people who had been injured by Bird had to wait up to 90 minutes before ambulances and paramedics came to their aid, despite numerous frantic calls to 999. Some witnesses were so frustrated by this they even took it upon themselves to drive the injured to hospital in their own cars.

Elsewhere, cafes and youth centres were converted into makeshift clinics, so that local GPs, fire-fighters and others with a knowledge of first-aid could assist the injured. And then there are the disturbing reports that some of the bodies of Bird's victims lay on the spot where they died for a matter of hours because of the lack of scene-of-crime officers on hand.

Barrie Walker, a local GP from Seascale, was one of the people who would call to question whether Cumbria was well enough equipped to deal with such a major trauma.

The GP, who works at the Seascale Heath Centre, tended to the wounded Harry Berger, who was shot in the shoulder and was treated at a makeshift clinic that had been set up in a youth centre. 'We're not Northern Ireland, we're not Moss Side [an inner-city area of Manchester],' he said, in an interview with the *Telegraph*. 'We're not used to dealing with a gunshot wound, a guy who's bleeding, losing his blood, and there's no ambulance coming for two hours. It's actually very difficult and you feel impotent.'

Dr Walker had been called out by neighbours after Berger's collision with Bird's car in Seascale. Berger, who had been shot in the shoulder, had survived the shooting but was, according to witnesses at the scene, in a huge amount of pain and was crying out. A witness reported that, 'It was extremely distressing as there was just nothing we or the doctor could do about that.' Numerous calls were made to the emergency services but it would be some time before an air ambulance arrived at the scene and ferried the wounded man to hospital.

According to reports over 20 paramedic vehicles and several air ambulances were on standby at various points to treat the wounded and injured. But for a large proportion of time the majority of these were held back by police and not allowed into areas where there were wounded – or even dead – because it is alleged that the police believed entry would be unsafe. In the case of Harry Berger, a witness claimed this was why there was such a delay in the air ambulance's arrival at Seascale.

By the time police did arrive, Bird – who by then had

already taken the lives of Michael Pike and Jane Robinson – had left the town ten minutes previously and was making his way towards the National Park. It also transpired that helicopters from the Great North Air Ambulance service were grounded by the police for safety reasons and were only allowed to fly when they were instructed that the coast was clear and they were in no danger. But, by that time, some of the injured had already been taken to hospital by members of the public.

'It was a horrible time for our guys, having to wait, knowing there were people out there critically injured,' a spokesperson for the Great North Air Ambulance said. 'But could you imagine what would happen if one of our helicopters came in to land? I'm sure he would have shot at the aircraft. The police did not let them fly but we were happy with that. Their safety is paramount. We had a consultant and a paramedic in each helicopter, one was an army doctor. One aircraft was dispatched to three locations but the victims had already been taken to hospital.'

Dr Walker has since said that the delay in getting paramedics to the scenes could have cost lives. 'I find it very strange that I and another doctor were able to treat the injured man, but emergency personnel were not allowed through,' he said. 'After all, the danger had moved away from us by that time but we saw neither police or ambulance staff. Eventually, armed officers from Sellafield, from the Civil Nuclear Police, did arrive, but it was an hour before an air ambulance turned up to take the man to hospital. Fortunately the delay did not have any major consequences for that man – but it may have done for others. When this whole incident is considered afterwards, questions need to be asked about getting help to people more quickly.'

Witnesses say that there were similar scenes in Wilton, where Bird shot Jennifer and James Jackson. Neighbours remark that whilst Jennifer Jackson died instantly from her gun wound her husband Jimmy was alive for some time but was losing blood. 'Jimmy was alive for a while after he was shot but an ambulance couldn't get to him because people were worried that the paramedics might be shot too,' they said. 'I can't imagine what he went through.'

One of the injured women, Jacqui Lewis, who suffered a head wound when Bird shot at her in Drigg – near to where he killed Jane Robinson and Michael Pike – had to wait on the roadside for over an hour until police came to her aid. A local who stayed by her side said, 'We didn't see a police car for nearly an hour after the shooting. Everyone was calling 999, and Bird had clearly moved on, but no on came,' he said, adding that in the end the pensioner had to be taken to hospital in a police car, as they couldn't get an ambulance to her.

In scenes that caused further distress some say they were both concerned and upset about the amount of time it took for some of the bodies to be removed from the streets, especially in Seascale. Two witnesses and Dr Walker, who was called to the scene, having treated Berger, claimed that it wasn't until 9pm at night that the bodies of Michael Pike and Jane Robinson were attended to because there weren't enough scene-of-crime officers on the ground, as referred to previously.

Tony Whillock, a resident in Seascale also questioned why it was that the emergency services at Sellafield hadn't played a more responsive role. The nuclear plant has an extensive emergency unit of its own, with helicopters and air ambulances, but because it had been locked down it would be some hours before they were able to respond to the incident. Whillock, an Oxford academic, called them time and time again but could get no response. '[They] could have sent an ambulance straight there almost immediately –the plant is only ten minutes away,' the disgruntled resident said. 'It was the only ambulance for miles. I rang them several times but 90 minutes passed before they gave the go-ahead. When the ambulance eventually arrived from Sellafield, an air ambulance was already there, so it was of no use,' He added that the local community was furious because of the lack of response.

A spokesperson for the North West Ambulance Service would later defend the delays, arguing that the safety of their crews was 'paramount'. Answering Dr Walker's criticisms she said: 'We can't take our advice on safety from a GP – though we were very glad he was there. We have to listen to the police. Two dead paramedics wouldn't be much use to anyone.'

Perhaps lessons do need to be learned from what happened that day in Cumbria. For there do seem to be issues over both the co-ordination and communication between the emergency services that morning. But once again this was an 'exceptional incident, in exceptional circumstances' and as Dr Walker himself conceded, 'To see this kind of carnage in the gutters, in the streets... there was blood running in the streets of Seascale – is just something you don't expect.'

CHAPTER SEVENTEEN

One week after the shootings, with inquests opened and then formally adjourned, David Roberts, Coroner for North and West Cumbria, released the bodies of the 12 victims to their families so that they could lay them to rest. Twelve lives, twelve victims, twelve funerals. Twelve innocent people violently and brutally taken from this world by Derrick Bird for no apparent reason. Now at least they would find their peace.

After the very public show of mourning during the vigils and the memorials these funerals would be private affairs. The news crews, the cameramen, the journalists and photographers, the satellite vans had long since rolled out of town to allow these people the peace and quiet to mourn their dead alone. Each service would be personal and poignant, filled with as many tears as laughter, as their friends and family mourned their loved ones, paid tribute to their achievements and merits and celebrated their lives.

Each funeral was well attended, so much so that people often spilled out into the cemeteries or gardens of the churches and crematoriums. Each one was distinctive, like the people they commemorated. And each had a touch of the personal – whether it was in the music that was played, the hymns and the readings that were chosen, the eulogies that were given, or the items that were placed by their coffins, such as the tiny hand-made paper pigeon that perched on top of Jane Robinson's casket. Each interment was different, special, but if there was one theme that ran through them all then it was the fact that each of these people had been taken from life too soon, and at a moment in time when they still had too much not just to live for, but to give.

For the mourners themselves it was never going to be easy saying farewell to friends and family but they would do so with dignity and love. And for many of them it was going to be a difficult week, since in the case of some they weren't just attending one funeral but as many as three or four. And for the churches and crematoriums and for the local vicars they would conduct multiple services during that period. But each person who was laid to rest, each of Derrick Bird's twelve victims would be given the send-offs that they deserved. The community would once again rally together to give their loves ones the support they needed as they lined the streets, packed the churches and crematoriums and paid tribute to the people they had lost in such tragic circumstances.

One of the first funerals to take place was that of Gary Purdham, the rugby-playing father of two, who was very much regarded as a local hero.

Amongst the many tributes that were left for Gary on the gate of the Gosforth farm where he fell was an Egremont Rangers shirt that could be seen blowing in the breeze. It was the club where he had begun his rugby career. Next to it was a simple but poignant note written by his young wife Ros, that said: 'Gar, Daddy and Gaggy [sic]. Words will never express how much we love you. Always be with us – Ros and your wonderful boys.'

From his parents came the following words: 'Our beautiful son, taken from us in the prime of life. We will miss you so much.' Another note from a friend describes Purdham as a 'wonderful husband and daddy, a smashing son, a true hero and a legend in rugby league.' In the weeks that followed, his life would be celebrated and paid tribute to at rugby matches all over the country.

A thousand mourners would join Ros at Gary's funeral, which was held at St Mary's Church in Gosforth, and because there wasn't enough room for them all inside, hundreds of them would listen to the service via loudspeakers outside.

Ros, 35, arrived at the church with her youngest son in her arms, and holding the older boy by the hand. They were both dressed in pink Whitehaven Rugby shirts with their father's name emblazoned on the back. Gary's brother Robert, captain of the Harlequins rugby team, was a pallbearer and the coffin had been decorated with a floral tribute in the shape of a rugby ball.

In a tearful eulogy to the rugby player and family man Ros promised her husband that she would look after his boys and make him proud and said that it had been a 'privilege' to have been married to the man she described as her soul mate.

'Gary was kind, loyal and generous,' she said. 'We got married and it was the best party ever. We were such a close family unit and time was treasured and precious. Kisses and cuddles were always on offer without asking for them. The short time we had as a family is the best time we will ever have. Gary was and is the best friend I have ever had. I am so lucky that out of all the people in the world he chose me.'

Within hours of news filtering out that Darren Rewcastle had been killed Duke Street would become a shrine to him. Candles were lit, flowers laid, messages of love and support to his family were left. One floral tribute that was left came with a card that read: 'RIP Darren "The Chancer" Rewcastle.' Another said: 'Cruelly taken from us on this day that will be remembered as a tragedy. Sadly missed and never forgotten. I hope you have taken that great sense of humour with you.' The following day a large flower arrangement of red-and-white carnations – in recognition of his passion for football and the England team – was left at the rank.

On the morning of Darren's funeral 30 cab drivers would follow his cortege along the A595 to Distington Crematorium, where his funeral service was due to take place. They would be joined by a fleet of others waiting outside, each of them flying the England flag from their cars. It was a gesture they knew Darren would have appreciated and he would have liked the fact that so many of the mourners chose to wear football shirts to the service. They had even draped his coffin in the flag of St George. 'Happy, funny and cheeky' was how friends said Darren should be remembered. Over 400 people attended the service.

Susan Hughes was a much loved member of her community and this was very much reflected in the outpouring of grief that followed her passing. Colleagues and friends simply couldn't believe that such a kind and caring woman had been taken from them in such a violent way. 'We miss you so much and can't believe what has happened. God bless you,' read the card that had been left from a dance group of children and their mothers, which Susan had been involved with. Another from the ABC Nursery simply said: 'Thinking and caring'.

The mother-of-two's funeral service was held St Mary and Michael's Church in Egremont. Her daughters Melinda and Sarah had left a floral tribute of lilies, daisies and roses. 'To Mam,' the card read. 'Simply the best. In our hearts for ever.' As her coffin was led into the church, over 50 red, white and turquoise balloons were released by mourners into the sky. They were said to represent love and peace, and also Susan's birthstone, which was turquoise.

During the service Reverend Barbara Jeapes read out a eulogy from Susan's family. 'There are no words to describe our utter grief and devastation at the sudden, cruel and unnecessary loss of Susan,' it said. 'We remember her as a dedicated mother to her two daughters but she was more than a mother to them, she was also their best friend.'

There were many messages of love and grief left at the spot where Kenneth Fishburn died in Egremont. Amongst the flowers was a note from the staff at Ladbrokes, the betting shop, where Fishburn liked to have a flutter or two. They would later lay a wreath for him outside their shop, but this message would be left within hours of him dying: 'Miss you forever, your girls and Marc. Ladbrokes.' The message is perhaps all the more poignant now that we know that Fishburn was making his way to the bookmakers not in order to place a bet, but because he had heard about the shootings and wanted to check that the girls who worked there were all right. He may have retired from the forces many years before, but he would always be a soldier at heart.

Another tribute to Kenneth had been left by a stranger. 'I did not know you,' it simply read. 'But I witnessed your tragedy. May God rest your soul.' Kenneth's funeral was held at Distington Crematorium, which was filled with family, friends and neighbours, determined to give a fitting send-off for their 'army' man.

At the point where Isaac 'Spike' Dixon fell on a country lane leading to Carleton Wood, bunches of flowers were tied to the fence. But of all the tributes left there for him the most poignant of all was a wire mole trap – a simple yet fitting tribute to the much-loved countryman and part-time mole catcher. A week later 500 mourners attended his funeral, which took place at St Michael and St Mary's Church, in Egremont.

Fellow countrymen, local farmers, members of the Egremont Conservative Club, neighbours and some of the elderly whom Spike looked after, crowded into the church to join his sons Martin and Wayne, and his girlfriend Pat for the service. Describing their father as a 'warm and funny man' his sons paid tribute to Spike's unerring sense of generosity, whilst Pat left flowers for her partner with a card that read: 'Sleep tight Spike.' Speaking after the service a neighbour said that the community had just said good-bye to one of the most 'decent, kind and warm-hearted of men in the county' a 'true gentleman'.

As well loved and much valued members of their village and their parish, the deaths of Jennifer and Jimmy Jackson left the people of Wilton and Haile heartbroken. The couple, who had been married for 45 years, and died within just 150 yards of each other, had been stalwarts of their community and this was transparently obvious from the many messages of condolence that had been left for them. Amongst the many tributes left for the couple was a black-and-white photograph, taken on their wedding day.

After they died their family – led by son Christopher and daughter Kathryn – paid tribute to them, saying: 'They were a wonderful, quiet, loving people who were right at the heart of their community.' Expressing their shock at what had happened and explaining that they were trying to come to terms with the tragedy, they thanked everyone for their support. 'Everyone is in shock at this tragedy, trying to make sense of all that has happened,' they said. 'The community is close-knit and helps each other in tragedy.'

Jennifer and Jimmy Jackson were buried together after a packed funeral service in Egremont. Friends remembered Jennifer as being a gifted gardener who would happily lend her talents to the parish, whether she was tending to the church garden or arranging flowers for the services. As we know, Jimmy had dedicated his life to working for the ambulance service and had been Chief Station Officer at Keswick and Barrow. 'They were just an everyday people,' a neighbour said. 'Really friendly and always happy to pass the time of day. They were well known locally and had lived in the village a long time. There were none better.'

Their funeral service was conducted by Reverend Richard Lee and Reverend Barbara Jeapes. Reverend Jeapes knew Jennifer well through her work with the church and saw her every Sunday. 'James and Jennifer worked well together,' she said. 'Their deaths have left a hole in the community and there is a tremendous sense of shock. We have a community in mourning. Jennifer was quiet, determined, elegant and dignified. James enjoyed rugby, where he was known as "Jimmy". He liked the banter and the jokes. They touched the lives of so many people. We will miss them so much.'

Of all the tributes that had been paid to Michael Pike the most poignant of all came from his wife Sheena, who wanted to celebrate 'a life lived to the full'. 'Michael had a happy retirement walking, cycling, playing with his model railway, and was very happy and contented right up to the moment of his death,' she said. 'I take great comfort from his swift but too-early end and celebrate a life lived to the full. He was a clever, loquacious, loving man. A loyal and loving husband, father and grandfather. He was interested in so many things, engineering, the arts, politics and world affairs. Thank you Mike for all you gave us; you were very loved and will be very missed.'

Michael Pike was a committed Humanist and his funeral, which again was held at Distington Crematorium, was led by Jan Duckley, a celebrant of the British Humanist Association, who remembered him as 'A happy and fulfilled man at peace with the world and his place in it,' adding, 'He would have been amazed and delighted at the number of people who have taken the time to write or phone.'

His family – son Jason and daughter Jude – were keen that his funeral should be a celebration of his life, rather than a reflection on how or why he died, and as the congregation listened to John Lennon's *Imagine* they were asked to remember him in their own way. Summing up his own recollections of his father Jason Pike said: 'I have fond memories of him playing at being animals with us, especially lions, and of him taking us out swimming or the many picnics in the car. I only vaguely remember sitting on his last motorbike while it was standing in our garden; he sold it because a car would be more useful to the family.'

Five hundred people would attend the funeral of Jane Robinson at St Cuthbert's Church, in Seascale, to say goodbye to her. As well as her love for animals and birds Jane was passionate about music, which was reflected throughout the service from the hymns and other works chosen, to the presence of the West Cumberland Choral Society, which both Jane and her sister Barrie had been members of. They also sang carols, as Jane had always loved Christmas.

The service was led by her friend Reverend John Woolock, who had postponed his holiday in order to be there. 'We can't think of Jane without thinking of her and Barrie together,' he told the congregation. 'As I thought about their life together some of the words that came to mind were industrious, integrity, earnest and compassion.'

'Jane worked hard at everything she undertook,' Reverend Woolock continued, 'not least her care for birds and wildlife. She had strong views and beliefs but would listen to others. She also had great concern and compassion for people around her and for all living creatures.' Also there to pay tribute to Jane was her uncle Andrew Robinson who spoke of the 'twinkle' in her eye and her 'infectious laughter'.

The funeral of lawyer Kevin Commons took place on the day Prince Charles visited West Cumbria. It was held at St John, The Evangelist Church in Workington and over 200 people attended, with much of the congregation – many of whom were colleagues from the legal profession – all dressed sombrely in black. The 45-minute service, which was followed by a private cremation, was said to be a 'show of respect and support for the family'. Kevin's wife Helen led the mourners in the celebration of Commons's life, during which he was remembered for his sense of philanthropy and the generosity of his spirit. And after the hymn *Praise My Soul, the King of Heaven* – which was said to be one of Kevin's favourites – Tim Frost, a senior partner in his legal firm, gave a eulogy.

This was followed by an address by Canon John Kelly, a close friend of Mr Commons. 'What can we say in the face of such horror and tragedy that took place days ago, which led to the killings of Kevin and eleven other people in this locality, as well as those who were seriously injured?' he asked. 'The sheer magnitude of what happened on that fateful day defies belief. And I realise that a man or woman of the cloth faces a hiding-to-nothing as they stand up and offer any words of condolence in this situation.'

Printed on the Order of Service was a picture of a Lakeland scene. Below it was a quote by DH Lawrence. It read: 'The Dead don't die, they look on and help.'

Jamie Clark, the youngest of Derrick Bird's victims, was the last to be buried. New to West Cumbria his funeral would take place in Bedfordshire, where the 23-year-old had grown up. Ahead of the funeral his parents Richard and Jane, and Jamie's brother Andrew, had paid tribute to the estate agent: 'Dear Jamie, our son, we are all proud of you. Your happiness put sunshine in everyone's lives.' His father Richard said: 'Jamie was a happy-go-lucky, fun-loving person. He never hurt anybody.' His mother added: 'He had a wicked sense of humour. He was one of those people who made you feel better about knowing him.'

One hundred and twenty mourners, including Jamie's fiancée Leanne, took their places at the Vale Crematorium in Stopsley, Luton. Amongst the congregation were former school and childhood friends, as well as colleagues from the West Cumbrian lettings office where he worked. Speaking before the funeral his father said that saying goodbye to his beloved younger son was going to be one of the hardest things that he had ever done in his life.

Remembering Jamie, Richard said: 'I think it's all the little things he used to do. His love of *Star Wars*. He liked science fictiony [sic] things, he liked technology. In some respects he was a lot like me. And he enjoyed doing some of the things I used to do and that's what gave us such a good friendship. As well as him being a son, we could talk about things on the same wavelength.'

'I don't think I am ever going to understand,' Richard Clark said of the tragedy itself and of Derrick Bird's actions. 'Something happened and he has gone over the top. You can't blame his family for any of that. That is down to the individual. What he did is horrific. I have nothing against the family. They have offered to apologise but they don't need to. I have been through all the emotions and I don't know where I stand. We are never going to forget Jamie. The funeral is the hardest thing I have ever had to do in my life.'

Leanne Jarman spoke of how Jamie had a 'bucket list of things' he wanted to do before he died. Aside from marrying her he had wanted to make his first million, own a parrot and were they to have children she said that he had wanted to name his first son Anakin after a character from *Star Wars* — which, of course, will never happen now.

'I will never forget that day,' Leanne said. 'It was the worst day of my life. I screamed down the phone when I heard. Jamie and I had a future ahead of us. We were getting married and we were going to get a mortgage. So I have gone from being completely excited about my future to being terrified of it. Completely terrified of how I'm going to manage without him. It's never going to stop hurting.'

CHAPTER EIGHTEEN

At St Michael's Church in Lamplugh over 400 mourners would come to pay their last respects to David Bird. Indeed, so many people had come to say goodbye that the great majority of them were forced to stand in the graveyard and listen to the service through loudspeakers. Leading the cortege to the church was the digger that David had operated during his work. It was to be followed by his favourite Land Rover, which he had nicknamed Wobbly Tom.

His three daughters, Rachel, Tracey and Katie, were escorted into the church by their mother Susan. Behind them followed Graeme Bird with his wife Victoria by his side. The family vowed that they would not be torn apart by the tragedy. If ever there was a display of unity, then this was it.

Then came the coffin. It had been decorated with a floral tribute of his yellow digger. This was a personal touch that on an otherwise sombre day raised a smile from all who knew David and were aware of his lifelong passion for diggers and cars.

The service was conducted by the Reverend Jim Marshall and, as a family friend, he knew what to say as he gave his eulogy, which was both emotional and humorous. He recalled how David first met Susan as a teenager, their courtship and marriage in 1980. He spoke of David's love for his family, describing the joy and pleasure he derived from being a father to his three daughters. And of his love for dogs, recounting how he used to hide potatoes for one his favourites – Robson – so he could spend the day searching for the spuds, piling them up on the landing for his master to see when he returned home from work.

And Rev Marshall spoke of David's eccentric side and his sense of humour. How there was nothing that he liked more than a practical joke. Simple stories, small anecdotes, but ones which were heartfelt and meant the world to everyone there. Conjuring up a picture of this popular man he said: 'David is no longer standing beside us, cap, pipe and Day-Glo jacket at the ready.' As well as tears there would be wry smiles and ripples of laughter from the congregation at times. David Bird's life may have been cut short but he had led it to the full, Marshall said. He had packed a 'great deal into those 52 years'.

Reverend Marshall said that he had asked people close

to David to sum him up in one word. But following a barrage of adjectives he had to stop them and ask them the same question again. 'One word came out – "unique",' he said. 'To top it all they added "a legend". David was so loved by his family, loved by all those who knew him. Not because he was the lovey-dovey sort of dad, the cry-on-your-shoulder friend, but because he was unique. He was able to lift people's spirits in an unusual and affectionate way. He was able to express his love in his action and in his humour. And, yes, he was a legend because only he could do those things and get away with it – be famous for it.'

David's three daughters paid tribute to their father, words which were read out in church for them. They described David Bird as a 'one-in-a-billion dad', 'hilarious', 'quirky', 'cheeky and downright cute'. The girls' eulogy continued: 'You brought laughter wherever you went and always put a smile on everyone's face. With all these stories you will never die, with new stories coming everyday in our hearts you will always stay. So "put kettle on father", we'll see you soon. We can't put into words how much we love and miss you. Sleep tight, Dad, love, your girls.'

To the song 'You Raise Me Up', David Bird's coffin was carried out of church.

Still in hospital, Mary Bird was unable to attend the funeral and so a duplicate service was conducted by the hospital chaplain, Margaret Goddard, in her room. It would follow Rev Marshall's Order of Service word-for-word.

By the afternoon of Friday 18 June, following the funeral of Jamie Clark, which had taken place that morning, each of his twelve victims had been laid to rest. Twelve lives remembered, celebrated and mourned. Twelve people who would be loved and cherished in the hearts of their family and friends forever.

But the total number of people who died on 2 June 2010 was not 12, it was 13. For on that fateful day Derrick Bird would also call time on his own life, finally turning the gun, which had killed and maimed so many, on himself. And now it was time for his own family to say goodbye to him.

They had kept the time and the location of the funeral of Derrick Bird secret until the last moment and had held it last out of respect for the other families but on the afternoon of 18 June, the family and what friends he had left, bade goodbye to Derrick Bird during a private funeral at Distington Crematorium.

The service was again conducted by Rev Marshall and was attended by 100 people. Amongst the mourners were his sons Jamie and Graeme, with the latter's wife Victoria, and Derrick's brother Brian. The party, which included Bird's former partner Linda Mills – who held the arm of her son Jamie – arrived at the crematorium together in a coach, so as to avoid too much attention. As they made their way into the building many hid their faces from the photographers and journalists gathered outside.

As she was still in hospital, Mary Bird did not attend; once again the funeral service would be conducted to her at her bedside. Also absent were the daughters of David Bird: Rachel, Tracey and Katie. Earlier, they had expressed a wish to attend it, as a show of support for their cousins, but at the eleventh hour the girls changed their minds, saying that it was just too much for them. In a statement they said: 'We send our love and support to our grandma, auntie and uncle and cousins on this difficult day. As you can imagine this has been a very hard time for our family and at this present moment we do not feel physically and emotionally strong enough to attend the funeral. However, we would like to express our love and support to the rest of the family.'

Some who had known Bird for many years and who had considered him to be a friend simply couldn't face the notion of paying their last respects to a man who had caused so much damage. But there were those who decided to put those feelings aside for the day and say goodbye to the man they had known for 52 years, as opposed to the man he became on 2 June. One such person was Paul Wilson, the cab driver Bird had not only aimed a gun at, but had shot in the cheek. In the run-up to the funeral Wilson said he would be there because he wanted to say goodbye. 'He was my friend,' he said simply. 'I should be there.'

As a mark of respect to the families of Bird's twelve victims the family had insisted that his funeral, which was conducted by Rev Marshall, should take place last. Just before the service began Marshall said of Derrick Bird: 'I've described endlessly to people about the good man, the nice man, the loving and caring man that he was. And on that day, that dreadful day, there was another man doing the things that he did.'

Rev Marshall said he hoped that this final funeral service would bring a sense of hope and unity back to the community.

There would only be one address during the service and that was given by one of Derrick Bird's oldest friends, Keith Wilkinson who said that he first met Derrick when they attended the village school together in 1969.

'Inevitably we have to grow up,' he said. 'Who would know that one day someone so very close to us would break down, his mind lost to darkness and despair, and would be the cause of so much tragedy. If this affliction could snap a steady man like him it begs a question, "could it happen to one of us?" There but for the grace of God go I.'

After the service Brian Spencer, a family friend, read a statement from Graeme and Jamie. It said simply: 'Derrick was many things to many people but to us he was just Dad. To us he was a loving and caring family man, well-known and well respected in our local community.

'We will never understand what was going through his mind on Wednesday, 2 June, or why he killed and injured so many people. All we can say is that we are utterly devastated by his actions and deeply saddened by the legacy of pain he has left behind. Our love, thoughts and sympathies are with the families who are suffering at this time. We will miss our dad greatly and hope that we, along with all the families who have been impacted by this crime, can somehow try to move on and try to rebuild our lives.'

CHAPTER NINETEEN

With their loved ones finally laid to rest the families and friends of the twelve victims of Derrick Bird would go back to their lives and try somehow to rebuild their worlds, but it was never going to be easy for any of them.

Throughout the ordeal they had conducted themselves with dignity and courage. Not a single angry word had been voiced, not a sign of contempt towards Derrick Bird was shown. Instead they kept their suffering and emotions to themselves. They had mourned their loved ones collectively, side by side, at the vigils and the memorials. They had stood tall and proud at their funerals, and celebrated the lives of their brethren with a mixture of tears and laughter.

But now each of the families and friends of Derrick Bird's

victims would have to face the future with someone missing from their lives, someone who should be there for them, by their side. In their home, with their families, at their social clubs, their places of work, on the other end of the telephone, in their beds. Be there for them at birthdays, Christmases, on holiday.

When Derrick Bird took the life of Kevin Commons not only did he make a widow of his wife, Helen, but he deprived the community of a hugely philanthropic character. A solicitor who made it his business to help people, whether they could afford his services or not, was a rarity in his profession, some might say. He was also a successful businessman who lent his mind and his acumen to helping the good of the community. He was a man who lived his life for others.

In shooting 43-year-old Darren Rewcastle, Bird not only killed a man in the prime of his life but deprived his 14-year-old daughter Savannah of a future with her father. He would no longer be there to celebrate her successes in life, to be there when she needed him, to mark those special occasions – passing her driving test, her first job, her wedding or the birth of a child. He took a much-loved son from his parents and a good friend away from his colleagues. Without Darren there would no longer be so much impromptu laughter and tomfoolery down at the rank on Duke Street.

By ending the life of Susan Hughes he stole a mother from her two daughters Melinda and Doreen, who, as someone with severe disabilities, relied on that relationship. Susan, they say, was an exemplary mother, who prided herself on that role. But she didn't just look out for own, she had dedicated her life to caring for others. She worked with the disabled and was a much-valued and loved member at the centre where she worked.

Kenneth Fishburn, a former soldier, had given – and risked – his life for his country and his family were proud of that. He had worked as an enforcer of the peace for the UN, and as such was someone who wanted to make this world a better place. He was not a man that should have been taken from it.

Jimmy and Jennifer Jackson were community-minded people. Jennifer volunteered for the church, and Jimmy dedicated his working life to the ambulance service. They were parents and grandparents who delighted in that role and loved being with their family. Tragically, they no longer have that pleasure.

Isaac 'Spike' Dixon was also a family man and had a partner, Pat. He was a countryman, one who would think nothing of helping out a farming friend or someone in need. He cared for the elderly in his neighbourhood, bringing them eggs, running errands for them, doing odd jobs. Who will do these kindnesses now?

When Derrick Bird shot Gary Purdham he killed a much-respected sportsman, a man who knew the meaning of being part of a team, rather than thinking of himself first and foremost. The killer left Gary's wife without a husband at a tragically young age. He deprived Gary's two young sons of ever getting to know their father, leaving them with just a handful of memories.

Jamie Clark, recently engaged, was entering a new chapter in his life. He had a job that he loved and was good at, and a fiancée, Leanne, whom he adored. The couple had planned to marry the following year. Thanks to Derrick Bird, Leanne will never have the pleasure of calling Jamie her husband now. In the killing the 23-year-old he broke the hearts of Jamie's parents and of the rest of his family, who had many hopes for him.

Michael Pike knew how to live life to the full even in his retirement. At an age when most people like to slow things down he filled his days to the brim. He cycled, he read, he followed politics, he walked the fells. He was also someone who worked for the good of others, having represented his trade union when working at Sellafield. He was also a loving family man who adored spending time with his children and their families.

And then there was Jane Robinson, the kind, gentle and selfless woman who had devoted her life to caring for animals and birds. As such, Jane was someone who saw the value in life, whether she was rescuing animals or simply feeding the birds along the promenade at Seascale. She had lived all her life with her twin sister Barrie, with whom she shared a home. By killing Jane, Derrick Bird took away the person closest to Barrie Robinson.

So there were more than just twelve victims that day… there were, in fact, hundreds: the people who have lost their loves ones and have been left behind. For them nothing will ever be the same again. They have lost children, brothers and sisters, husbands and wives, mothers and fathers, grandparents, colleagues and friends, a fiancé. For them there will always be someone missing in their lives: an empty chair at a table, a familiar face missing from a family photograph, the person they spoke to last thing at night and first thing in the morning.

In time, these hidden victims might learn to heal themselves, they might slowly begin to be able to rebuild their lives but there will always be a void there. But it wasn't only these people's lives that Derrick Bird destroyed. He devastated his own family as well, causing them not just pain and suffering but feelings of confusion too.

By murdering his own brother Derrick Bird took away a loving father from his own nieces and deprived their children of a grandfather – a role friends say David Bird was born for. He robbed Brian Bird of his younger brother and his mother Mary of a son, and, as if that wasn't enough in itself, he turned the gun on himself – repeating the whole process all over again.

Derrick Bird may have ended his life as a cold-blooded killer but, as stated previously, for 52 years he had been a much-loved son and brother. A different man, those closest to him have said. And he was also a father.

Graeme and Jamie Bird loved their father very much and he was an integral part of their lives. But by killing himself, Derrick Bird put an end to that. He will no longer be at the sidelines cheering Graeme on as he competes at Motocross. He won't be around to take Jamie diving or be at his side when he learns of his exam results and he won't be there to see his grandson Leighton grow up. That was his choice, but it was not that of his sons.

At the time of writing this book, we reflect that the past few weeks cannot have been easy for either Graeme or Jamie but Derrick Bird's sons have behaved with extreme dignity and strength in the face of these difficult circumstances. Though 'devastated' by his father's death Graeme was determined that he and his brother should be the ones to organise their father's funeral. According to Rev Marshall, who has kept in close contact with the boys, Graeme wanted to take on that role, having just become a father himself. 'Since then he has become a man who feels a huge sense of responsibility,' Rev Marshall said.

In the meantime, despite being given a dispensation to miss his exams, Jamie Bird completed his GCSEs. The 16-year-old, who is said to be academically gifted, was resolute in his decision to take his qualifications, much to his mother's and his school's pride and admiration.

For the rest of their lives Graeme and Jamie will have to live with the sins of their father, but like the other families who suffered at his hands they will also mourn someone they loved. For these two young men there will also be that empty space at the table, that person missing from the family photo, the familiar voice at the end of the telephone.

In the eyes of the rest of the world Derrick Bird may be a brutal and cold-blooded killer but to them he was simply just 'Dad'.

CHAPTER TWENTY

Derrick Bird will never stand trial for his crimes. Having taken his own life in the woodland of the National Park that day he passed judgement upon himself and decided his own fate. Whilst there are some who no doubt think that the world is a better place without him, for others his suicide is problematic on many levels. Unlike the people he killed on 2 June Derrick Bird chose to die that day. He was able to select the time and the place where his life would end, a choice that was not afforded to any of his 12 victims.

And by committing suicide, which some would see as the easy way out, Derrick Bird has also denied the families and friends of the victims their day in court. For as painful and harrowing as a trial would be for them, at the very least it would have given these poor bereaved people the chance to discover the truth, to answer the many questions that must haunt them day and night.

Derrick Bird deprived these folk this form of closure when he took his life. Instead it is now left to the Cumbrian Police Force to step into the breach and find out the truth for them. And they have pledged to the people of West Cumbria that they are committed to do so. No stone will be left unturned, they have told them. They will investigate every avenue of enquiry, they will examine every single piece of evidence, follow every lead they have, no matter how small. They have vowed to do everything they can to getting to the bottom of what really happened on 2 June 2010, because they know that people need answers. The police understand that, because they are part of this community themselves.

It is, however, not going to be an easy task for them. Derrick Bird left a multitude of crime scenes in the wake of his rampage through the West Cumbrian countryside. He had a multitude of motives which led him to kill, all of which need to be investigated. There are the testimonials of the hundreds of people that Bird had dealings with to go through. Interviews have to be conducted, witness statements have to be gone through, his possessions need to be carefully examined, his paperwork, his finances – and those of his family – will be analysed. It is an investigation that begins in the tiny hamlet of Rowrah but will take them as far afield as Pattaya, Thailand. Every aspect of the killer's life will come under scrutiny, for only then will they be able to present a true picture of what happened that day.

As the Cumbrian Police have said, this really is an exceptional case and one that will require a great deal of manpower and resources, which has been recognised in Westminster. In the week that the Chancellor of the Exchequer George Osborne announced a series of widespread cuts across the board as part of his emergency budget, the new government pledged financial support for the Cumbrian Police Force.

In a debate in the House of Commons towards the end of June, Home Office Minister James Brokenshire announced that a request for extra money for the Cumbrian police would be backed, explaining that the case was complex and would need extra resources. 'The government will support any bid from Cumbrian Police for a special grant to help its exceptional costs on the force budget,' he said.

'They've already received some specialist support from neighbouring forces, for example police helicopters and scenes-of-crime officers.' But he reiterated David Cameron's views that any review on the gun laws would only come once the police investigation has been fully completed, which he admitted could take time. 'Witnesses are still coming forward and the investigation is going to take many months to complete. Whilst I recognise the desire for answers, it's important that the investigation takes its proper course.'

Since the shootings, and at the time of writing this book, that investigation has been well under way. Paperwork and computer hard drives that have been removed from Derrick

Bird's house are now being painstakingly scrutinised. Derrick Bird's finances and his tax issues are being looked into, as are the alleged family disputes over inheritance and money. The police have also been in contact with the killer's GP, and have looked into his medical records, although it is believed that there is no record of Bird having any mental health issues. Nor did he apparently have any history of depression, and he had never been prescribed any form of mind-altering medication, such as antidepressants. Family, friends, neighbours and colleagues have also been spoken to at length.

Detective Chief Superintendent Iain Goulding of the Cumbria Police said that they were 'absolutely determined' to get to the bottom of why Derrick Bird chose to kill twelve people and injure a further 25 on that fateful morning; but he admitted that they may never find satisfactory answers, as they can never speak to the man responsible.

'We may never know why,' he said. 'In a case like this the only things that can provide clear answers as to what was on the killer's mind is some kind of suicide note. We are satisfied now that there was nothing left by him to explain what he did.'

With Derrick Bird taking his secrets with him to the grave, when he pulled the gun on himself, it is now up to detectives to unravel his story and find a motive. Accordingly they have been closely looking at the four main areas they believe hold the key to his crimes: his relationships, his financial problems, the grievances he had at work and family issues.

'They are focusing on several key areas and working to verify suggestions that Bird was involved with personal disputes with fellow taxi drivers or others,' Goulding said. 'We have also been reviewing his finances and investigating issues of taxation. We can confirm that Bird was subject to an ongoing investigation by Her Majesty's Revenue and Customs.'

But whilst Derrick Bird may not have left a suicide note the police may be able to gain further clues as to what was going through his mind that day, as it has been reported that the killer made contact with a number of people in the final moments of his life.

According to a report in the *Daily Express* Bird made a series of calls to family members and friends, moments before he took his life in the woods, apparently telling them: 'I've done something really, really bad.'

Having quietly told them what he had done, he is said to have ignored their pleas to turn himself in and hung up on them. It is claimed that Bird, who refused to answer repeated calls from the police earlier on his own mobile phone during the spree, telephoned friends and family member from three pay-as-you go mobiles, which the police have been trying locate in the dense undergrowth of the woodland. A family friend who lives close to Mary Bird in Ennerdale told the newspaper that Bird realised then there was no turning back. 'He made calls before he killed himself. He said he'd done something really, really bad. Obviously the enormity of what he'd done had begun to sink in,' they said. 'It's a terrible tragedy. If he'd lost his mind during the shooting it was back in gear when he was in that wood. He knew there was no way out.'

Minutes after his final call, Derrick Bird would commit suicide.

The Daily Express also quoted a police source who is said to have told them: 'Any information will assist the coroner in compiling a complete picture of what was going through his mind when he embarked on this appalling course of behaviour. We are aware he made phone calls before taking his own life. But we are not sure how many and to whom. We know about some but suspect there may have been more. He may have tried to phone some people who did not respond.'

Having been granted extra resources, and since an extensive team of detectives have been appointed to the case, the investigation promises to be a thorough one; but that is not to say that the police don't have their work cut out for them. As Goulding said they are 'faced with simultaneously investigating 12 murders and 11 attempted murders' which is not an easy task. But police have said they are as resolute in trying to get some answers as they are determined that the events of 2 June 2010 should not be repeated again.

Submitting an initial report into the case to the Cumbrian Police Authority, Chief Constable Craig Mackey was in agreement with Goulding's stance on the situation, admitting that it could take many months as police continue to piece together not only what had happened that day, but to try to find out what had led to it in the first place.

'This case was probably unique in British policing,' Mr Mackey said. 'We had 30 crime scenes across 45 miles, with hundreds of witnesses. The search of the route took 24 hours. The question families and the community want to know is why. We want to be able to answer that but we are realistic – we might never be able to give that complete answer but it won't be for want of trying. We are very keen to look at what we can learn from these unprecedented incidents that will help Cumbria and the national debate.'

In the meantime Tim Farron, the MP for Westmoreland and Lonsdale, has called for a public enquiry into the shootings. 'It goes without saying that there will be no trial, and that is why a full – and I would say public – inquiry is crucial, on terms set, as has already been said, by the community,' Mr Farron said in a parliamentary debate. He also argued against the notion that the forces of Cumbria should be merged with those in Lancashire, an idea which has been open to debate for some time, saying that some political and interested parties were using the shootings as an excuse to bring the merger forward. 'Some of the patronising stuff written in the media focused on Cumbria being a pitifully small county with a police force that cannot deal with its problems,' he said. 'That is nonsense.'

It's a view that seems to be shared by the majority of West Cumbrians themselves, who are said to be angered by a lot of the criticism directed towards their emergency services in response to the shootings. As far as the majority are concerned both the police and the ambulance service behaved in an exemplary manner and, as such, have not only paid tribute to them but have started raising money for both. At some of the funerals of the victims, rather than ask for flowers, many of the families suggested that donations be made to the emergency services instead.

The people of West Cumbria may never be able to answer the question as to why one of their own would want to turn on them on that morning in June. They may never understand why a middle-aged man who seemed on the face it to be such a kind, nice and sociable person, a person they considered to be part of their community, and a 'true Cumbrian' would want to wreak so much chaos, confusion and carnage across their streets and lives. They will never really know why anyone would harm so many lives. In killing himself in the secluded woodland of the National Park, Derrick Bird deprived them of that knowledge.

If anyone was angered by that during the weeks that followed the shootings they didn't let on. They didn't demand answers to questions, they didn't criticise the role that the police or the emergency services played on the day, and they didn't clamour on the door of 10 Downing Street demanding a repeal of the gun laws. They refused to cast any stones and would blame no one – not even Derrick Bird himself.

Instead they pulled together as a community and faced their tragedy, their loss and pain as one. Despite all that they have had to endure in recent years – the cost and the loss that was caused by the floods, the agony of the coach crash in which they lost two teenagers and now the shootings – they stood side-by-side and vowed to get through this together. And whilst they wouldn't, couldn't, forget what they had been through, they looked forward, as if to say they wouldn't be defined by it all.

CHAPTER
TWENTY-ONE

There is perhaps one further victim in this tragedy that has yet to be mentioned, and that is West Cumbria itself. Having already suffered at the hands of the floods, losing a beloved and respected policeman in their wake, having had to endure the tragedy of a terrible coach crash the month before, in which two young lives were taken, could this region and its people really cope with any more heartache and suffering?

There are some that worry that the actions of Derrick Bird will taint the good name of this beautiful and once peaceful part of the country forever. That the name of West Cumbria and its towns and villages will no longer be associated with the green and pleasant land that it is, but instead be synonymous with the violent and brutal actions of one man on one day. As resident Barrie Moss, the man who tried to come to the aid of Susan Hughes as she lay dying, observed ruefully: 'The name of Whitehaven is forever ruined. If you talk about Whitehaven, it's going to be associated with Columbine, Dunblane and Hungerford. It's never going to be "it's a lovely place come and see". And this guy has done that to these people. He has changed everyone's lives forever.'

Moss was talking about his own town of Whitehaven but he could have just as easily have been referring to Seascale, Egremont, Wilton, Boot – any of the places within the 43-mile radius where Bird pulled the trigger of his gun.

But places, like people, do move on in time. They may not forget, they may not forgive, but they grow and they heal.

For the residents or Hungerford, Dunblane and Columbine, having the name of their towns associated with that of a massacre, or a killer, hasn't been easy. Prior to the shootings they had been known for being an attractive market town, a peaceful cathedral city and a friendly middle-class suburb respectively. But following the events of a single day in their history, they would be known for something else; for a violent attack, for the loss of life, for the actions of their spree killers. Trying to move away from that, trying to re-establish their identity, was always going to be difficult. As Ron Tarry, the former Mayor of Hungerford explained: 'Wherever you go, when you say you're from Hungerford, people think of Michael Ryan, a man with the gun. It just gives the wrong impression of the friendly place that it is.'

But over the years the people of Hungerford have done

their best to try and re-establish their town in the minds of others. Whilst they appreciate that the name of Hungerford will always be associated with that of Michael Ryan, especially in the aftermath of a spree killing, they also want the name of the town to conjure up other images as well – of an attractive market town, a warm and friendly community, a place where people would like to come and visit. The community there realise they can't eradicate their history but they have learnt to accept it, and have tried to move away from it over time.

Similarly in Dunblane, they, too, have learnt to take a step forward. They will never be able to forget what happened that day, for it would be impossible to do so anyway, it is not something that any of them want to dwell on. They will always cherish the memories of the ones they have lost and will never forget them, but have tried to distance themselves from the crime itself.

Andy Murray, the tennis star, was a pupil at the primary school where Thomas Hamilton carried out his rampage in Dunblane and he had been there on the day. When he first arrived on the tennis scene Murray was dubbed the 'boy from Dunblane' and would be persistently asked about it in interviews. Journalists who interviewed him during that time wouldn't ask him how it felt to win the Junior US Open; instead they asked him how it felt to be at school when a crazed gunman opened fire. But at the time Andy Murray refused to be drawn on this, saying simply that he was too young to remember.

Only recently has the young tennis player finally felt comfortable talking about what happened in Dunblane that day. In his autobiography *Hitting Back*, Murray writes of his recollections of that morning and how he, then aged eight, and his fellow classmates, were ushered into their headmaster's office and told to hide under his desk until the ordeal ended. Murray explained that whilst he only had impressions of that day, he had known Thomas Hamilton as a child, as he and his older brother Jamie had once been members of his boys' club. This was what he felt was so disturbing – this was why he couldn't look back, as it was something his 'brain couldn't cope with'. Murray would only reflect on that day in his own time, when he was ready to do so, and that is how many others who were touched by the events in Dunblane feel today.

When *they* talk of Dunblane, they are not referring to Thomas Hamilton's deadly deeds but of their home town. A place where they grew up, went to school, worked, socialised, got married, had their children and, as such, it is understandable why they don't want their town simply to be linked to a crime, no matter how atrocious it was. And so, like the people of Hungerford, they strive for people to see their town in other ways.

It can't have been easy for Andy Murray to be known as the 'Boy from Dunblane' at the beginning of his tennis career, for he knew all the negative connotations that came with that description. But aside from wanting to be known for his ability on the court instead, there was another reason why Murray tried to distance himself from all that.

This was because, as he has alluded to in the past, he wasn't the only child there that day.

There were other people affected by the tragedy. People who lost sons and daughters, brothers and sisters and friends – people Murray knew well. So with this in mind he didn't want to become the poster-boy for the tragedy. But it is thanks to Murray's and his brother Jamie's incredible achievements on the tennis circuit over the past few years that Dunblane is now recognised for more positive reasons these days than simply for a massacre.

It has since emerged that family and friends of those who suffered and lost loved ones in both Dunblane and Hungerford have privately come forward to the people of West Cumbria and offered their support and guidance as to how to come through the tragedy as best they can. It has also transpired that authorities in Hungerford have contacted their counterparts in West Cumbria to lend them support. The councils of Hungerford and West Berkshire have pledged to do all that they can to help Whitehaven and its surrounding areas to turn the corner. Ron Tarry said that the events had brought back painful memories for a lot of people from the area and, because of this, they were willing to do anything they could to help.

'It all sounded too much like Michael Ryan,' Mr Tarry said, referring back to his town's tragedy. 'On the first day it was just absolutely numb but the next day people thought something has to be done. People didn't want to talk about it in the immediate aftermath. It's part of our history that they are not particularly proud of. There was a great community spirit here which I'm sure there will be in Whitehaven and people wanted to help,' he explained. 'Hungerford was a quite a small town, like Whitehaven, and that spirit must be kept together.'

Likewise the authorities in Dunblane have also said they would be on hand to help the area move on. No doubt the people of West Cumbria will appreciate these gestures, for only those who have lived through these rarefied experiences will really know what it is like to have to live through and deal with such a tragedy.

In all that has been written about the West Cumbrians through all their recent tragedies there is one description that keeps coming up over and over again, and that is they, as a community, are 'close-knit' and despite all that they have been through it is this spirit that will pull them through the ordeal. The fact that this is a community where 'everyone knows everyone' will no doubt serve as a great comfort to the people there. As the Bishop of Cumbria had said when he addressed the congregation at that first vigil in Whitehaven, just days after the shootings and referred to West Cumbrians as being 'tough as teak, gentle as lamb': 'The sharing of each other's burden will be crucial to the healing of each other's communities in the long run.'

This was certainly apparent in the cases of Dunblane and Hungerford, where locals rallied together to support one another. In each community people rallied round each other for support. For the people of Hungerford this was crucial, for one has to remember that nothing like this had ever occurred in this country before. Doctors, nurses and teachers from the local schools set up support groups. Counsellors and therapists in the area would offer their services free of charge. Neighbours started to keep an eye out for one another.

'The community changed overnight,' a former townsman said. 'We'd always been a friendly and neighbourly people but after that it was different. When you stopped someone on the street and asked "How are you?" it was no longer just a greeting, you actually meant it. It's quite amazing how people come together. This wasn't just one person's tragedy, it was a collective one, we all felt it.'

In Dunblane similar things occurred. Drop-in centres were opened, support groups were started and at the town's social club they collected all the toys, flowers, presents and messages of support and distributed them through the community. 'It was a strange time. People stopped thinking about themselves so much, it was all about helping each other,' a local said. 'Neighbours were always asking after each other, cooking for one another, helping out with chores and all that. I think we all felt so helpless in one way but needed to do something because of that feeling.'

As Charles Clysdale, who lost his five-year-old daughter Victoria in Dunblane, observed in an interview with the BBC: 'The community really came together. Families who previously didn't want to know one another were bringing cards and gifts. It was really quite uplifting. We formed parents' groups and it gave us a chance to talk. We were all there for the same reason and as the weeks went on, we got quite friendly and came through it together.'

It is this sense of community that has helped other areas survive similar tragedies. In Port Arthur, Tasmania, where Michael Bryant killed 35, the locals have pulled together as a force to help one another and a year after Dunblane they invited some of the parents who had been affected by their own massacre to Tasmania to spend time with them and to visit their memorial.

In Columbine, parents' and students' groups were set up, not just by therapists or psychologists, but by the communities themselves. 'We felt strange discussing our issues with strangers, on our own,' a former pupil of Columbine said. 'I remember thinking in one session "What do you know about how I feel? Have you ever had a school friend of yours shoot at you? Have you witnessed your friends get shot?" It didn't matter to me how qualified the shrink was and I'm sure she meant well but at the end of the day I just wanted to sit down and talk with people who had actually been there on the day, who knew what I was going through. Even if we didn't actually discuss what happened it just felt comfortable being in a room with them.'

It is too early to say how the people of West Cumbria will want to commemorate their loved ones, although many have already expressed a desire to create a permanent memorial to them. Following Dunblane the gymnasium at the primary school was demolished and in its place the townspeople, school children and staff there, erected a memorial and created a garden of remembrance.

In Columbine they, too, pulled down their library and their cafeteria, and on a hill above the playing fields and the basketball courts they erected a granite monument, which is engraved with the names of all those they lost that day. And on 20 April every year the High School now closes for the day as a mark of respect to those who died on that date.

In Port Arthur they have also erected a monument in memory of those they lost, this time in the form of a cross, and they built a memorial pool, which lies in the shadow of the ruins of what was the Broken Arrow Café. Visitors on tours of Port Arthur are given the history of the prison but no reference of the massacre is ever made. This is something that is never mentioned to outsiders. It is their private tragedy and they prefer to keep it that way.

It is uncertain yet as to whether the authorities and the locals will want to demolish Derrick Bird's house in Rowrah. This has been done in the past to prevent 'souvenir hunters' and ghoulish visitors from visiting the homes of killers – notably in the case of Gloucester serial killers Fred and Rosemary West. Demolition was also carried out in the cases of Columbine and Dunblane, where school rooms were torn down. However, Bird didn't actually harm anyone within his home, so it may well be that such action isn't necessary, and for the moment his house stands, its windows and doors boarded up.

The general consensus amongst the locals is that they

need to have time to heal and grieve before they make any decisions on anything like that. 'It's too soon for us to even begin to think about what we want to do,' a local said. 'I think we all need some time to breathe. The families who have lost people need time to deal with their emotions and all the rest of us can do is be on hand for them in their time of need. Not by making grand gestures, it's the little things that count. But one thing we can do is start getting this area back on its feet again. It's the summer, we have tourists and holidaymakers here, we have things to work towards, we have to keep going – for each other.'

The people of West Cumbria may not have a memorial yet but for now they have each other and they will survive this latest tragedy, just as they have withstood the terrible events that have gone before – its people will make sure of that. They have their memories, many of which are undoubtedly dark, but they also recognise that they have to look forward.

And so on a hot weekend in the last week of June the locals came together again. Not to mourn this time, not to attend vigils, memorials or funerals but to celebrate, gathering together in their thousands to attend the annual food and music festival in Whitehaven. There had been questions as to whether the festival, which was in its twelfth year, should be postponed as a mark of respect. But in the end the general consensus amongst both the organisers and the community was that it should go ahead, with many believing that it would lift the spirits of not just Whitehaven but of the region as a whole.